I-SFI Insider's Edition

SOCIAL MEDIA
MARKETING STRATEGY

the BEST all-in-one HOW-TO guide on

**Marketing Strategy | Social Media | Content Marketing
Inbound Marketing | Networks & SEO | Social Selling**

ALEX ABAZ

Facebook | Google | Instagram | LinkedIn | ... | Pinterest | Twitter | YouTube

*Traffic & Links, Followers & Communication, Conversion
Marketing, Organic Reach, Analytics, & Advertising*

Other Books by Alex Abaz

1 The Go-to Book on Google+: Social Media Marketing & Social Networking plus Google+ {Google My Business} for dummies & brands
2 Cut to the Chase! The best sites to learn how to buy and sell online
3 Cost Comparison for Advertising and Reviews – Kindle Edition
4 Cost comparison for Digital Downloading of Images and Media
5 Catch the Spark Within: Transform a mere existence into joy-filled authentic life
6 Inside the Polar Vortex of An Arctic Winter Blast: Collection of Photographs and Inspirational Verses

For information and special offers please contact Alex Abaz:

Email: so.o.good.productions@gmail.com.

Twitter: @Alex_Abaz

Facebook: facebook.com/Alex.Abaz.Author

Google+: google.com/+SooGoodAlex

Google: sites.google.com/site/publishdigitally/

This book is dedicated to my son Brad whose strength of character and positive disposition makes me swell with pride. I know his future is bright because his talents are many and his goals are set high. Thank you Brad for helping me with the cover.

ISBN 978-0-9881053-4-8

Message from the Author ~ Alex Abaz

WOW! You're checking out my book, which means that my marketing is working. This book can definitely help YOU with your social media marketing strategy. My goal is to give you the best all-in-one how-to guide and make it easy to apply. The book has a lot to offer whether you're a blogger, a small business entrepreneur, or a big brand marketer. It's a valuable resource for the beginner and experienced marketer. "Social Media Marketing Strategy" delivers 95+ scoops of expert knowledge and outlines various ways for you to succeed online.

This is the first volume in the "I-SPY Insider's Edition" series. It focuses on using the internet as the cornerstone of your marketing strategy, outlines best practices for promotion via social networks and your website, and specifies how to measure and analyze results or yield. You'll learn about which network is best for your purposes, how to craft content for engagement, and how to optimize for search and get traffic to your website. Ultimately, the end goal of any marketing strategy is to generate leads and sign-up customers, and the key to that is conversion marketing and sales acceleration. Rest assured that I've been there and I know what you need to achieve your goals.

As a business executive and entrepreneur, I've worked with the best people building the latest technology, creating direct marketing campaigns, and selling to CEO's of major organizations. I've produced sales brochures and learning aids, built websites, organized major conferences, and exhibited at various trade shows. I have built companies from the ground up in several sectors and I am passionate about entrepreneurship. Those are my qualifications but I don't expect you to rely solely on my know-how. I'm serving up insider tips and solutions revealed by top advertising and marketing executives. I hope that inspires you to buy this book and put the 95+ scoops of expert advice into practice. It's a wise investment.

As an added bonus, I will be pleased to email you an enhanced version of this book in pdf format. Read more about this free offer at the end of the book. Also, if you would like to place a bulk order and receive an author's discount, please contact me. It's a great resource for everyone in your business.

Best regards @Alex_Abaz

Table of Contents

95+ Scoops of Expert Advice

Introduction

This book will help you with online marketing strategy and social media networking. It's a big topic but I get down to the nitty gritty on content, style of interaction, networks and search considerations. It explains different marketing tactics and elaborates on the art of engagement for the purpose of gaining leads. What do you need to know about social media and marketing to sell your products and services, collect opinion and customer satisfaction data, create content marketing assets, and drive traffic to your website?

You are no longer limited to traditional methods of marketing and advertising. Social media platforms give you the tools to discover your target audience and engage with them person-to-person. With these tools you can become a marketer with significant influence. Not only can you reach people but you can also track their actions from post to post. Not only can you address your message to an individual but you can create content for a multilingual audience. You can target a local niche or a mass market. You have access to market data that is granular and can be filtered, and can look at metrics for insight into the big picture and the specifics. If you are a small business or self-employed, with a small budget, you don't have to hire a marketing or public relations firm to do press releases, conduct focus groups, and organize events. If you are a large corporation, you can take control of your brand marketing and loyalty programs.

Sometimes we forget that it's not enough to have an awesome product. People have to know about it. As a marketer your job is to create awareness and give them the incentive to take the next step. Success hinges on developing a marketing machine that is fueled by great content and lean practices. Promotion takes as much strategic thinking as the product creation itself. Your marketing strategy has to combine both inbound marketing tactics and automation. How do you attract people to your offers and drive them to sign up? Having an understanding of how best to promote your product – whether it is with social media, email outreach, backlink building, or syndication – allows you to develop a winning strategy.

The process is straightforward. First attract people to your offer, next engage them, and then drive them to a form where you can capture their data. Once you fill up the top of the funnel with leads, marketing automation nurtures and converts them to business.

In this book I share what I know to be true about marketing and networking after many years in the business, and what I've learned from gurus and influencers through my research. The book is a condensed version of hundreds of blogs, and research and surveys, sifted with a business mindset and summarized for quick learning. There is something in this book for the beginner and the advanced user, and I believe it's an awesome resource that will give you lots of ideas and marketing insight. With 95+ scoops of knowledge, you can create content that engages followers and converts leads to customers.

Social Media Marketing Strategy delivers 95+ scoops of expert advice from top knowledge workers. Think of it this way – they're all on your team without being on your payroll. To get the most from this book, read it from start to finish and then return to

---

* Words & phrases underlined (links) are cross-referenced with URL addresses at the back

certain scoops when you need specific information. The itemized list of 95+ scoops will make it easy to find what you need when you need it. I should mention that I had a hard time splitting topics into sections. Inbound and outbound marketing, search and links, content marketing and engagement, all have to be considered together when formulating a marketing strategy. You'll want to read the entire book to get every scoop. Best wishes for success in all your endeavors.

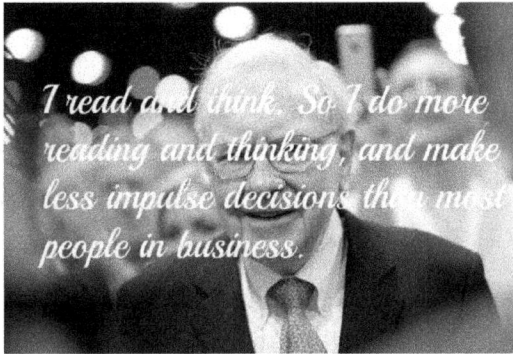

I read and think. So I do more reading and thinking, and make less impulse decisions than most people in business.

Permission Marketing & the Post

Scoop #1: The post

Information is power. Every like (+1), share, and comment on a post or tweet tells you who you are resonating with. When you know who that person is, you can start to build a relationship with them. Additional sifting and engagement allows you to find your brand advocates and connect with the influencers in your niche. You can support, encourage, and reward people's actions in ways that are meaningful to them. You don't have to rely solely on coupons and reward points. Marketing is all about connecting with people's feelings and developing trust. Posts allow you to do that. Everyone is special and every post interaction is unique. Social media makes it easy to connect with people and make them feel special. Every thank you note you post can be personal even if you're speaking to a group. Posts have the allure of a Hallmark card and the volume of a media channel.

Scoop #2: The magic of posts & +post ads

There is so much you can do with posts. Each post is a forum for interaction in real time, which can be crafted for each application. The fact that Google has revamped its' advertising program to take advantage of posts, tells you something. The +Post Ad is

Google's latest advertising option and a fundamental shift away from pay-per-click ads. Posts have so much inherent value that Google is using them to get marketers to upgrade from pay-per-click ads to pay-per-engagement. Twitter and Facebook have also come out with post templates that push advertising campaigns. With posts, you can wave your magic wand and get real engagement. Martin Shervington's blog on "Getting your Google Brand Page ready for +Post Ad" at *plusyourbusiness.com* is an excellent resource on Google's +Post Ads.

Scoop #3: Posting – how to get the most from a post

Social media platforms give you the tools for social engagement but you need to learn how to best deploy them for your purposes. This is what you need to know to get the most from a post:

1. How to optimize each post to encourage the most engagement
2. When and where to share it within the network
3. How to build Google+ engager circles, Facebook friends lists/circles, and Twitter lists
4. How to comment and stay on brand, yet encourage engagement
5. How to deal with issues that may arise on post threads

Scoop #4: Permission marketing

Social media has taken "permission marketing" to the next level. You no longer have to ask for people's email address. You have a personal file on them, starting with their Profile, their on-line trail of likes and shares, YouTube videos, hangouts, and events, and specifics from their posts as to what they're all about. You can learn about their interests, their status, their followers, their family and friends, their pets, their location, where they like to vacation, what they like to read, their preferences, and their customers. You can speak to people directly especially when they engage with you first. Once you connect with someone with a tweet or a post, they've opened the door and invited you in. It's about relationship building and it's done over many interactions.

Seth Godin explains what "permission marketing" is in his post at *sethgodin.typepad.com*. Permission marketing is very different from how advertising and promotion has been done before. It boils down to the notion that the customer has choices and can choose to ignore ads and propaganda. A person can decide what to engage in and when to do it. For that reason, they demand respect and consideration. They can subscribe to a blog and that's one way of giving permission to get notifications about future blogs. They can also unsubscribe quickly. Respect is earned and not demanded. It's earned with each like (+1), share, and comment. While this style of marketing may be slow to bear fruit, it is more effective and less costly than conventional channels. You don't have to pay to post once or 100 times.

Scoop #5: Circle curation & conversion

Your followers can become your customers if your content is taking account of their preferences and needs. Is your content resolving a problem for your engagement circle? By earning their respect, and becoming an authority on a topic or a person of influence in a sphere, they will come to you when they are ready to make a purchase. But that is only if you have been preaching the right message to each person in the choir. That presumes that

* Words & phrases underlined (links) are cross-referenced with URL addresses at the back

you have been paying attention to what your followers are saying and serving what they like. It also means that you are hand-picking the people for your content, i.e. curating the circle and matching content and delivery format to the target audience.

Scoop #6: Post optimization

How do you optimize your posts? A post that delivers a big punch will get better engagement than one that blends into the background, even if it's packed with great content. In order to fine tune your posts you have to use metrics that focus on key performance indicators (feedback signals). With most social-media posts you can easily judge the degree of success based on the number of comments, likes (+1), and shares. What do you have to do to make a post awesome?

- ✓ Create convincing post titles / headlines
- ✓ Give an interesting story
- ✓ Write meaningful post content
- ✓ Format your content
- ✓ Include a picture
- ✓ Always include a website link
- ✓ Give credit to other users
- ✓ Include hashtags
- ✓ Be engaging and responsive

All this is very doable as you'll see and there are tools and apps to help you do it well. But you only get a couple of seconds to catch the person's interest and get them to like (+1), share, comment or click on your post. While you can't control the person's psychology of behavior, you can influence them. By addressing a need with the right pitch, tone, and timing, research data shows that engagement goes up.

Crafting an awesome post takes hard work and then it may only get a short run. Susanna Gebauer writes that success is not certain even for pros and illustrates this with data from Upworthy. Some posts get lots of shares but no click-throughs, for example. (A click is not the same as a share.) It's not enough to come up with the right topic.

A post has to shout out to the person by combining an intriguing headline with an interesting image, teaser text, and a call to action. The same post content with a different headline can give you a much different result. That's why you have to put as much effort into coming up with the headline as you do crafting content. The title or headline cannot be an afterthought.

Generally, you want to create content that can be shared on any network, and use management apps to automate and schedule the publishing. But you also have to consider network restrictions and terms of use. Twitter for example, limits the number of characters per tweet to 140, while Google+ gives you enough space and features to turn every post into a mini-landing-page. By using Twitter cards, images & GIFs, and links, you can cheat and make more of every tweet. Nick Churick's blog titled, "How to Leave your Readers no Other Choice but to Tweet your Content" has five excellent tips for crafting Twitter posts that can be used to optimize all your posts on social media networks:

1. Come up with "magnetic headlines". That's the bait needed on each and every post but especially on Twitter posts, because the headline is essentially the entire tweet. A magnetic headline has to grab the follower's attention

---

* Words & phrases underlined (links) are cross-referenced with URL addresses at the back

instantly. (See also Scoop #92 on how to optimize the headline.)

2. Find a proven idea and use it as the foundation of your post. Research what types of posts get shared the most. You can use free social media analytics tools, discussed in the next section, to analyze engagement and see the number of impressions generated by a particular post. Nick Churick suggests using a tool called Content Explorer to see "how many times the relevant content has been shared via different social networks. Just type in the keywords and phrases you've been thinking of".

3. Share something useful that makes the person retweeting look good. Most people will retweet something useful because it "allows people to position themselves as wise and experienced buddies in the eyes of their followers". Nick says that useful content promotes itself.

4. Create shareable visuals and tweetable quotes to enable easy sharing. Nick's tip is to use tools that make it easy for followers to share your content. For sharing visuals on WordPress, install a Shareaholic plugin or a Singpic plugin, as they are simple to use. For tweetable quotes use Click to Tweet and TweetDis plugins for WordPress.

5. Ask for what you need e.g. help, retweet, RT, visit. A simple request at the beginning or end of your tweet will prompt followers to share your post. Research data on retweets-per-follower by HubSpot shows you can increase your retweets substantially with a call-to-action phrase. The one that got the most retweets said it straight out, "Please Help". Nick's best tip is to just ask for what you want.

6. Pin your favorite post to the top of all your social-media profiles and pages. Twitter, Facebook and Google+ all have

this awesome tool, which you can access through a drop-down menu on every post. Make it easy for followers to find something to share quickly. If they have to go on a scavenger hunt, chances are they'll retweet the first thing they see. I'm surprised at how many people don't have anything pinned. This is my best tip of the day for how to push the post you want retweeted the most.

7. Add a caption to every post you retweet or re-share. It gives your brand more visibility and improves search and ranking for your content. Adding your own hashtags or calling out to people can also extend your reach. By doing this, you are using someone else's content to rack up impressions. That's like riding on someone else's dime. The caption should be relevant to the initial content.

Continue reading for more scoops of expert advice on how to optimize different elements of a post. For example, Scoop #14 outlines best tips for optimizing Google+ posts.

Scoop #7: Post real estate & image size

Another useful tip on how to optimize your posts to make them jump off the page has to do with image size. You want to size your images so they fill the entire picture frame based on the custom dimensions set out by the social media network for posts. That means you want to take up as much real estate space as possible. What you don't want is to present a thumbnail visual if it's at all avoidable. That's what happens often when you share a link in a post. The image gets cut to a postage stamp. Even if this gets you more reach on Facebook, for example, people won't necessarily engage with it because it doesn't draw them in. You'll have to test and weigh options and possibly make tradeoffs.

* Words & phrases underlined (links) are cross-referenced with URL addresses at the back

Have you noticed that some images on Google+ are much larger than others? With Google+ you can upload images in the original size and have them displayed in large format. Prepare your photos for uploading using the aspect ratio specified by Google+. Thanks to smileywar.com for specifying aspect ratios that are best for sharing images on Facebook, Twitter, and Google+.

Facebook: Aspect ratio = **1.92**
e.g. 1,000 width x 521 height (pixels)

Twitter: There are two aspect ratios:
Summary large image= **2**
e.g. 1,000 width x 500 height (pixels)
Summary image: Square
Smallest is 120 width x 120 height (pixels)

Google+: Aspect ratio = **1.67**
e.g. 1,000 width x 599 height (pixels)
Hangout on Air banner
e.g. 1,200 width x 300 height (pixels)

How big should your photo be? A width of 800 to 1,000 pixels gives the best showing on small and large screen devices.

Use the formula: **Height = Width / Aspect Ratio** to calculate proportions and come up with the actual size of the image.

The aspect ratio for Facebook is 1.92
Twitter has two formats with only one aspect ratio of 2
Google+ uses an aspect ratio of 1.67

For example, on Google+ if your image width is 1,000 pixels divide that by 1.67 to get a height of 599 pixels.

Scoop #8: Animated GIFs

Animated images have become the craze on social networks. An animated GIF is an image that moves in a loop, which is created with a batch of images. Animated GIFs are commonly used by websites like Imgur, Google+, Twitter, Tumblr, Reddit, and BuzzFee. Animated GIFs have been around since the 1980s and have been making a comeback in recent years. They are popular in news articles, marketing campaigns, and art galleries. You can find animated GIFs online on sites like GIPHY.com or you can create your own by pasting a <u>video</u> URL into the <u>Imgur</u> "Video to GIF" Maker, for example.

A simple search can get you instructions on how to post GIFs on each platform. There's no question that attaching an animated GIF to your post can clinch it for you. For example, you could raise the interest factor for a cookie photo with a GIF of the "Cookie Monster".

Google+ gives you the option of animating the cover of your Profile or Page. That will impress and amuse your visitors. Matt Steiner says you can animate covers on both desktop and mobile devices. You'll need the dimensions for creating animated GIFs and these were published by Google in 2013:

- 497x150 pix = 135 frames (10064250 pix)
- 497 x 277 pix = 73 frames (10049837 pix)
- 497 x 300 pix = 68 frames (10138800 pix)
- 497 x 367 pix = 55 frames (10031945 pix)
- 497 x 250 pix = 101 frames (10100000 pix)
- 333 x 100 pix = 301 frames (10023300 pix)

Instagram supports multiple image formats, including GIFs. To post a GIF, select the file from your device instead of taking a

* Words & phrases underlined (links) are cross-referenced with URL addresses at the back

photo and upload it to Instagram. GIPHY offers a one-click solution to turn any GIF into a looped 15 second .mp4 for you to upload directly to Instagram.

Facebook now supports animated GIFs in the News Feed. You cannot upload GIFs from your computer or mobile device and cannot post them to Pages yet. If you try uploading from your computer, Facebook will convert it to a still image. You can embed GIFs in status updates by adding the link to the GIF. The link can be an Imgur link, a Google image search link, or any other link to a GIF. Your Auto-play settings determine whether the animated GIFs in your News Feed will be played automatically

Twitter supports animated GIFs that are looped. GIFs can be up to 3MB (Photos can be up to 5MB and GIF, JPEG, and PNG files are accepted. BMP or TIFF files are not accepted). Images are automatically scaled for display in your expanded tweet and in your user gallery. You can get instructions for uploading from Twitter Help. You can select up to four images to tweet at once but animated GIFS cannot be included in tweets with multiple images. Also, you can either tweet a GIPHY link or upload a GIF to Twitter directly from giphy.com.

Scoop #9: Promo posts on Facebook

In November 2014, Facebook announced new rules for their News Feed – no more promotional posts. Marketers have been posting ads on their pages for free organic reach, and Facebook wants it to stop.

> "As part of an ongoing survey we asked hundreds of thousands of people how they feel about the content in their News Feeds. People told us they wanted to see more stories from friends and Pages they care about, and less promotional content."

Facebook explains that "When people see content that's relevant to them, they're more likely to be engaged with News Feed, including stories from businesses." My understanding is that Facebook expects to reduce the volume of stories for a user from an average of 1,500 to about 300 daily.

Apparently, people are seeing more promotional posts on Pages they like rather than ads. That's because Facebook controls the number and quality of ads (based on engagement, hiding ads, etc.) a person sees in the News Feed but has not been monitoring promotional Page posts closely. That's now changed.

Facebook lists traits that make organic posts feel too promotional:
- Posts that solely push people to buy a product or install an app
- Posts that push people to enter promotions and sweepstakes with no real context
- Posts that reuse the exact same content from ads

It appears that some brands have been dripping their ads in the News Feed for double exposure. The content in a post cannot match an ad. A post cannot have promotional copy but it could promote a link to a website, for example. Sweepstakes contests may be okay as long as they offer "context".

Facebook warned that those "Pages that post promotional creative should expect their organic distribution to fall significantly over time." Facebook refers businesses to their <u>Page publishing tips and best practices</u>.

But Facebook has been changing the rules for the News Feed a lot lately and that has frustrated marketers who have seen organic reach drop dramatically (as you'll read in later sections). That's why they add "this update is part of a larger, <u>ongoing effort</u>. By

---

* Words & phrases underlined (links) are cross-referenced with URL addresses at the back

making News Feed more engaging for people — with Page post creative that is more relevant to them — we're also creating a better platform for businesses to reach their customers and find new ones."

Facebook maintains that Pages "offer a free, easy-to-maintain online presence for people to discover and learn about a business". The high traffic to Pages (over one billion) has Facebook exploring ways to build more features into Pages — messaging to communicate with a business directly, browsing video and photo content, customizing Pages based on industry, and onsite shopping. Facebook's course is clearly laid out and the game plan is that you have to pay to play. They maintain that "the majority of Pages will not be impacted by this change." That is hard to believe since promotional posts were quite popular.

Given all the controversy about reduced organic reach, I wondered why Facebook continues to enjoy solid popularity and revenue growth. Surely, if people were abandoning their accounts in droves as has been written, usage would drop and marketers would be disinclined to keep investing in Facebook. But that's not my take on it so I have to presume that the organic reach is enough to satisfy marketers. But how much is enough? I guess-estimated the organic reach based on recent reports of 1.25 billion active users and research data for engagement, which is presented in later scoops. If 44% of Friends Like posts at least once a day, that's a stream of 550,000,000 posts per day. What is the audience amplification potential? For Pages with over 100,000 Likes organic reach is at 5% and that is equal to a bandwidth of 5,000 to 27,500,000 posts (for accounts with 100,000 to 550,000,000 Friends). For Pages with less than 10,000 Likes organic reach is at 11% and that is equal to a bandwidth of 1,000 to 60,500,000 posts. What this indicates is that even if organic reach for each post has tanked, the amplification potential is large given the sheer number of active users, and that can translate into a lot of leads.

Alan Coleman agrees with my conclusion, "For reach, relevance and amplification potential, Facebook is unrivaled." His blog tips marketers on how to leverage this crowded platform to drive traffic to relevant content. An objective opinion from an expert like Alan can help you decide how to promote your content and where best to spend your advertising budget, "Adwords is still the best ad platform in the world for conversion. While Facebook can rival it for reach, relevance and CPCs it can't come close on conversion (in most cases)."

ISAI – Interaction Signals As Indicators

Scoop #10: Measuring interaction signals

To get the most engagement and optimize your marketing strategy you need data. You need to analyze what's working for you and what's not. Who is paying attention to your posts? Where should you invest more time? Which content is shared the most and by whom? Social media makes it easy because you can easily track Interaction Signals as Indicators (ISAI). Social media platforms like Twitter, Facebook, and Google+ have tools that you can use to gain insight and metrics. You need to study the reports on followers and posts to understand who you are resonating with. Refer to the end of this section for the scoop on dashboards, insights, and analytics tools available on the major social media networks. For example, you can get a free <u>Facebooks's competitive report</u> that compares up to 10 fan pages. There are other social media analytics tools, such as CircleCount, which is a favorite for Google+. You can use <u>Content Explorer</u> to analyze and compare sharing of relevant content among networks. Scoop #63 leads you to a big toolbox of social media apps and tools.

In a recent email, Twitter highlighted that their research indicates a high level of engagement by Twitter followers through retweeting especially.

> "Research shows that your Twitter followers are a valuable and engaged audience. 70% of them amplify your content for free by Retweeting it, and 43% plan to make multiple purchases from the small and medium sized-businesses they follow. As your follower base grows you gain more opportunities to drive these actions with every Tweet."

Social media is a fantastic promotional channel for your business and you can get on it for free. For example, it is estimated that on average 6,000 tweets appear every second on Twitter, which makes 360,000 tweets per minute, and 500,000 million tweets per day. Every tweet has the potential of being retweeted many times over, and that can bump up the click-through-rate for your campaigns. But to capitalize on the opportunities, you have to test, measure, and analyze. Which tweet generated the most impressions? What hashtags were used? How about your competitors? Your ISAI scores hold the answers.

Scoop #11: How to analyze post engagement

After you set up your Page you need to look at which posts are working and which aren't? "Google Plus Analytics and Insights" at plusyourbusiness.com, recommends using a tool such as "Steady Demand Pro". Which parameters do you need to tweak to get more traction? When you analyze engagement, you want to look at signal-to-post ratios, and also break down the post activity by day and by feedback signal – likes (+1), shares, re-shares, and comments. Come up with a score for connections, post quality, engagement, engagement by post type and time of day, and top engagers. Are you getting more circle "adds" on certain days? Look at the posts for that day. Does the length, formatting, or mentions change the signal? Are certain #hashtags casting a wider

---

* Words & phrases underlined (links) are cross-referenced with URL addresses at the back

net? Is there a time of day that gets better engagement? How does frequency of posting affect engagement. Also look at whether your brand is getting more mentions (+name). Which posts are scoring higher on what key signals? (More on this topic in later sections – e.g. see content analysis & attribution report.)

Scoop #12: Competitors' posts

You may also want to analyze the engagement of posts published by your competitors and influencers. What are they doing that you may want to consider replicating? Are their posts longer and do they have better infographics? Is the person posting someone with authority? I'm more bound to watch a video by Matt Cutt than someone I've never heard of before. Even if you're not able to replicate the activity, by analyzing you know the key signal at play. Dissect their posts and try to score them. Also look at their followers. What can you do to engage some of them?

Scoop #13: Key signals & Google search

What do you need to do to get on top of the Google Search page? Google looks for movement in a positive direction as far as engagement and growth of key signals without any major spikes. Google prefers gradual growth based on original content and strong engagement that is continuous and steady, rather than erratic activity.

Get more expert advice on this topic in Scoop #30 – Social factors critical to search rank.

Scoop #14: How to gain engagement, optimize posts & create community

Kevin Lee's blog, "Unlock the Power of Google+: 13 Ways to Gain Engagement, Optimize Posts and Create Community" at blog.bufferapp.com, is a fabulous bundled resource. Kevin' team at Buffer conducted tests to explore new ways to better engage with their audiences. Check out how they did their experiment and set up your own. Based on their findings and expert opinion they concluded that Google+ is a smart place for business to be.

The team at Buffer used various metrics to discover what made the most difference in engagement. Their results confirm what other studies show about the use of visual content, as discussed in later sections (e.g. Scoop #78). However Buffer reported on a couple of elements that I haven't seen any data for elsewhere. This is what they found:

- Asking questions boosts comments by 188%
- Including animated GIFS boosts likes (+1) by 39%
- Embedding videos boosts likes (+1) by 28.6%
- Adding quotation marks boosts likes (+1) by 16%
- Using images boosts likes (+1) by 9.4%

Based on their results, they came up with 13 ways you can boost engagement:

1. Post up to five times per day without losing engagement
2. Always start with a headline
3. Share the most popular content at the best time – by showing videos related to your business you can get roughly 29% more engagement; post on Fridays from 11 am to 2 pm
4. Show enthusiasm in your posts – Interesting content is not enough. Grab attention with: *YES! Finally! WOW! OMG!*

* Words & phrases underlined (links) are cross-referenced with URL addresses at the back

Whoa! Other factors that correlated to success were: breaking news, content demand, image use, simple message, optimal post time, re-shares by influencers, community impact

5. Take your blog comments to Google+ (or vice versa)
6. Embed your Google+ posts directly on your site – similar to Twitter and Facebook but with storyline
7. Make good use of Google+ hashtags – Google+ adds more hashtags for you automatically (blue highlight); those you add are highlighted on the side menu (gray highlight)
8. Connect your Google+ YouTube Page with your Google+ Page
9. Create a community and use circles creatively – tailor the updates you send and share with specific groups; communities are hugely important for relationship building; dig into these places daily and post your most relevant and well-timed content; comment
10. Share straight from Google Drive – share interesting forms, surveys, spreadsheets, how-to documents, and presentations by uploading from your disk drive
11. Try your hand at +Post ads – pay-per-engagement rather than pay-per-click
12. Use Author Rank to improve search rank for your website. Come up with good content and use great bylines. Google uses bylines to identify subject experts and boost them in search results
13. Try live video with Hangouts On Air – lots of tools for engagement: live presentations, multiple hosts, slides and visuals, and tools to engage with live audience; archived replay

Get more expert advice on this topic in later sections, and Scoop #78 – Content stream.

Scoop #15: Social networks – analytics tools for insight

Twitter, Facebook, and Google+ offer free analytics tools to help you gain followers and optimize engagement. You can also upgrade to get more metrics on your followers and invest in advertising campaigns. Google Analytics gives you granular data and is by far the most comprehensive. One of my favorite tools for Google+ engagement is Circle Count. Most of this information is available on the social sites. I've included it below for quick reference and to ensure you don't miss out.

Tweet Activity Dashboard: "When someone follows you on Twitter, they are choosing to stay connected to your business. Learning more about your followers such as their demographics and their unique interests can help you turn followers into paying customers." Twitter data shows you follower growth over time, locations of top followers, their interests, and who they follow. Twitter offers more stats for a fee to allow you to optimize your marketing strategy.

What is the Tweet Activity Dashboard?

The Tweet activity dashboard displays Tweet data to help you optimize your performance on Twitter. You can leverage these insights to inform ongoing content strategy for both paid and organic Tweets and content. Here are five questions the Tweet Activity Dashboard can help answer:

1. How many impressions do my tweets receive?
2. Which of my tweets resonate best with my target audience?

---

* Words & phrases underlined (links) are cross-referenced with URL addresses at the back

3. How do my tweet metrics break out by organic and promoted activity?
4. How does my recent performance compare to past results?
5. How do my engagement metrics breakdown by type?

How to use the dashboard:

✓ You must have access to Twitter Ads or Twitter Analytics to access the Tweet activity dashboard.

▪ Users can get access to **Twitter Ads** by signing up at *ads.twitter.com*

▪ Users can get access to **Twitter Analytics** by signing up at *analytics.twitter.com*
   On analytics.twitter.com: Select the Tweets tab

You may want to invest in Twitter ad campaigns to amplify the distribution of your content. Go to http://twitter.com/i/redirect. They explain the objective, targeting and budget. Twitter suggests you start by selecting a campaign based on your objective: website clicks or conversions, app installs or engagements, new followers, Tweet engagements, or leads. You then use their robust targeting options to reach your ideal customers based on their interests, demographics, device types, behaviors and more. Select or create a few Tweets to promote and set a budget. There's no minimum spend level and you'll only pay for the results that align to the campaign objective you've established. For example, in a Website clicks or conversions campaign, you'll only pay for clicks to visit your site from the Tweets in your campaign.

Facebook Insights: You can get information on your Facebook Pages and Audience. Page Insights shows performance data after at least 30 people like your Page. Find demographic data about your audience, and see how people are discovering and responding to <u>your posts</u>. Page and Audience insight don't always match because the number you see in Audience Insights is based on the number of people that are connected to your Page that have logged-in to Facebook in the past month, while the number of people you see in Page Insights is based on the total number of people who like your Page. (To access Facebook Page Insights log into your account, select your Page, and click on "Insights" from the top menu.)

Audience Insights lets you learn about your target audience so you can create more relevant content for them. With Audience Insights, you'll be able to see:

- Demographic information about your target audience, including trends about age and gender, relationship status, and job roles.
- Lifestyle and interest information about your target audience.
- Purchase information about your target audience, including online purchase behavior, which categories they're mostly likely to buy in, and location data that may help you identify where to run special promotions or host events.

To learn about an audience using Audience Insights: Go to <u>Audience Insights</u>. (To access your Audience Insights page you have to be logged into your Facebook account.) Then go to: www.facebook.com/ads/audience_insights/

In the screen that appears, choose an audience you want to look at. You can choose between everyone on Facebook, people connected to your Page or a Custom Audience:

- ✓ If you have multiple ad accounts, select the account you want to use from the drop-down at the top of the page.
- Use the filters on the left side to define your audience or use the interactive graphs to refine your audience.
- Click Save.
- Give your audience a name. You'll be able to <u>use your Audience to create an ad</u> in Power Editor.

Google Analytics: A powerful suite of real time and summary reports on metrics that allow you to understand your audience characteristics and identify new audience targeting opportunities. You can compare mobile conversion rates and target profitable geographic areas. You can customize your analytics dashboard and get alerts. Learn more about from <u>Google Analytics</u>.

Google Analytics provides a comprehensive set of best practices, techniques, and how-to's for:

1 Advertising and Campaign Performance
   - Advertising Reports
   - Campaign Measurement
   - Cost Data Import
   - Mobile Ads Measurement
   - Remarketing
   - Search Engine Optimization
2 Analysis and Testing
   - Advanced Segments
   - Annotations
   - Content Experiments
   - Custom Reports
   - Dashboards
   - Real-time Reporting
3 Audience Characteristics and Behavior
   - Audience Data & Reporting
   - Browser /OS
   - Custom Dimensions
   - Flow Visualization
   - Map Overlay
   - Mobile Traffic

- Social Reports
- Traffic Sources

4   Cross-device and cross-platform measurement
- Universal Analytics

5   Data Collection and Management
- API
- Filters
- User Permissions

6   Just for mobile apps
- App Profiles
- App-Specific Metrics and Dimensions
- Crash and Exception Reporting
- Google Play Integration
- IOS and Android SDKs

7   Product Integrations
- AdSense
- AdWords
- Google Display Network
- Google Tag Manager
- Google+
- Wildfire

8   Sales and Conversions
- Attribution Model Comparison Tool
- Data-Driven Attribution
- Ecommerce Reporting
- Goal Flow
- Goals
- Multi-Channel Funnels

9   Site and App Performance
- Alerts and Intelligence Events
- Event Tracking
- In-Page Analytics
- Site Search
- Site-Speed Analysis

There is also a dashboard for your Google+ Page, and it's under "My Business" in the G+ menu. It reports on post "Share", Insights for the last 30 days, and YouTube views. The dashboard gives you a snapshot and you can click to get more detail on posts, followers, engagement, etc.

---

* Words & phrases underlined (links) are cross-referenced with URL addresses at the back

CircleCount: This list is taken from, "10 brilliant things you can do with CircleCount" at *plusyourbusiness.com*:

1. Check the growth curve for followers, likes (+1), comments, shares, and re-shares
2. Analyze your public posts and score those posts that got the most engagement
3. Find the shared circles in which you have been included. How popular is your brand?
4. Manage your favorite posts
5. Create your custom ranking badge to see
   - the number of followers
   - the average number of comments, likes (+1), or re-shares per post
   - the country
   - profiles and/or pages
   - when last public post was done
   - the minimum number of characters per post
6. Use the Chrome extension to get additional information on any Google+ Profile or Page without having to leave Google+
7. Create a world map with your Followers
8. Manage your Google+ Pages as well as the Profile
9. Get a CircleCount badge for your Profile
10. Find interesting people, using filters for gender, country, and tags

Social Networks – Rank, Traffic & Links

Scoop #16: How to get traffic to your website

There are four ways to grow traffic depending on whether you take the short or long-term view:

1. Organic traffic – builds up naturally based on search engine optimization (SEO)
2. Referral traffic – also organic in nature but builds via articles or links
3. Paid traffic – buy keywords and ads with pay-per-click (PPC) or pay-per-impression (PPI) bids; requires keyword research and copywriting for your ads to entice visitors to click through
4. Direct traffic – word-of-mouth and off-line referral works best for well-known brands because visitors have bookmarked the site or are returning guests

If your website is new the quickest way is with paid traffic but you still need to augment it with referral and organic. As your brand gets better known, you want to focus on content to get return visitors and also impress other partner sites for link building. Over time, SEO will deliver free organic traffic. Ensure that your website is well designed and optimized, with landing pages and calls to

* Words & phrases underlined (links) are cross-referenced with URL addresses at the back

action. The site needs to be mobile friendly and tablet compatible, and responsive to different screen sizes. A site that is built with HTML5 provides a better user experience.

If you have a budget for paid traffic, you have options with PPC, banner and link promotion (e.g., Facebook PPC ads, Google AdWords, Stumbleupon.com, and BuySellads.com). Google AdWords has the best conversion rate. Keep your Ad group small initially and targeted, with a low daily budget. Start with one keyword and keep testing different ones. You may have to test 50 to 100 keywords. You can also try content network ads using the same approach. Use "enhanced bidding" and remove all websites with a low click-through-rate (CTR) based on your stats. It's important to test dozens of ads to get the best content network conversions. Over time, Google optimizes the placement of ads for relevant sites, which means more conversions and more traffic.

Social media marketing takes time but can be very effective for different campaigns. Viral campaigns using humor or shock posts and videos will get you a quick pop and the content doesn't have to be business related. You can also look into Open Graph API at developers.facebook.com/docs/sharing/opengraph.

When you leverage influencers on the internet, their opinions and recommendations can drive referral traffic to your site. Marketing tactics for driving referral traffic include:

1. Article marketing – blogs or weblogs that reflect knowledge and a brand's point of view
2. Infographic marketing – approach high-ranked blogs to feature your content in their newsletters or post it
3. Tribe marketing – build a tribe of marketers / bloggers

4. Social media groups – build your own or join an established group (closed groups get less spam)

Email marketing, PR and content marketing, and community building can work very well if done correctly. Comment on blogs and answer questions on quora.com and other forums. To build traffic consider a mix of tactics based on your analytics reports:

1. Social media contests – running contests are good for ecommerce or content websites
2. Guest blogging increases your website ranking with SEO
3. Create community – invite top customers to share what they know about your product
4. Optimize your website back-end (H tags, Alt, keywords)
5. Word of mouth – friends, local business, national business
6. Promotional and informational videos
7. Collaboration – banner exchanges, shared email lists
8. Local profiles – e.g., Yelp, Superpages
9. Affiliate marketing – partner to bring targeted traffic
10. Web-traffic boosters – websites bringing targeted visitors where you get unique IPs or visitors
11. Directory submissions – submit your website to different directories (free and paid)
12. Podcasts
13. Case studies, reports and trends
14. Interviews and features
15. How-to guides, PDFs and eBooks
16. Reviews and testimonials
17. Create internet tools - modules, plugins, and extensions

Scoop #17: PageRank – definition

PageRank is important when it comes to building traffic for your website and getting people to follow you, share your posts, and engage. The best definition I found for PageRank is the following, "PageRank can be thought of as a model of user behavior. We assume there is a "random surfer" who is given a web page at random and keeps clicking on links, never hitting "back" but eventually gets bored and starts on another random page. The probability that the random surfer visits a page is its PageRank". (Lawrence Page, 1998) It stands to reason that the more clicking the user has to do to get to your page, the lower the PageRank assigned to it by Google.

Scoop #18: How Google Plus SEO affects posts & search rank

The most interesting research I've seen on engagement signal and how it affects PageRank is presented by Joshua Berg in "How Google Plus SEO Affects Posts and Search Rank – G+ SEO 2014" at *realsmo.com*. A post gets a measure of PageRank authority, and a fresh Google+ post starts with the highest level of authority associated with its' homepage. According to Joshua, "Google+ posts that receive no engagement at all, even from high authority profiles, typically receive no observable ranking authority". Posts which received good or above average PageRank authority averaged 52 likes (+1), 10 comments, and 17 re-shares. Joshua notes that it is the re-shares that give the posts the most authority. These posts also retain higher authority over time. The 116 low-authority posts averaged 32 likes (+1), 5 comments, and 5 re-shares. Any posts with fewer than 3 re-shares, out of hundreds of posts analyzed on different profiles, had no PageRank authority.

Scoop #19: PageRank, posts & links

Based on the research presented by Joshua Berg at realsmo.com, if you're using Google+ posts as a way of link-building to try to boost PageRank for your site, it's not going to work. (Read more on link building below.) The Google+ stream is continuously diluted with new content and unless your post has high authority, its' PageRank will drop rapidly. Joshua recommends that you use posts as a way of engaging people and interacting. Share your content, see how people react to it, and think about ways that you can improve content. Joshua says that Google+ posts with high engagement can act like a rocket booster for your webpage or blog. Joshua notes that there are other ranking benefits from Google+ and Google Authorship for authors' content, which flow into their Profiles, still to be understood.

Scoop #20: Internal links – calls to action

WOW! You got people to visit your site. Now you want to engage them and persuade them to linger and enjoy what you have to offer. One way to do this is with internal links following Ayesha Anwar's advice: "7 Best Ways to Optimize Links to Get More Clicks by Readders" at bloggermentor.com. The time they spend on your site is one signal that can help your PageRank. More importantly, you want to convert this visit into an outcome. If you can get them to click on internal links that take them to other pages or more detailed information, you're scoring points. "These links are actually 'calls to action' that catch the attention of your visitors

* Words & phrases underlined (links) are cross-referenced with URL addresses at the back

and compel them to click on these links", says Ayesha Anwar. In her blog, she lists seven ways to get your visitors to click on links. For example:

1. Format your links with bolding, underlining, and different color.
2. Don't put, "Click here" but use keywords or relevant text instead. This generic style of anchor text washes through the SEO stream.
3. Put your important links at the start of the page.
4. Open all external links in a new window.
5. Look at which links get you the most clicks. Make more of them.

Scoop #21: Social media & search rank

The good news is that the more you engage and share on social networks, the higher your search rank score. Believe it or not, your Google+ Profile, Facebook page, and Twitter account, may show up before your webpage on Google Search. According to Jennifer Barry's blog, "14 Tips How Social Media Can Drive More Traffic to Your Website" at business2community.com, buyers may seek out your social accounts before they check your website. Make the most of the "About" space to drive traffic from these social pages to your website. Make sure your brand is consistent across all your platforms.

Get more expert advice on this topic in Scoop #30 – Social factors critical to search rank.

Scoop #22: Which social network?

How do you know which social network is best for you? Is it Google+, Facebook or Twitter? Jennifer Barry's blog at business2community.com, advises to "go where your followers are". Consider who's going to buy your product. Just because Facebook is the largest network, doesn't mean you'll get your customers there. What really matters is conversion. Figure out where your followers are and then post according to their needs and preferences. You also can't dismiss networks with fewer followers and focus only on one platform. It may be that Google+ or Pinterest drives more business your way.

Scoop #23: Network comparisons

A chart by *Forrester* on the top 20 social platforms compares changes in active users. It shows that Google+ is even with Twitter, as the number two social network behind Facebook. And there is positive growth for Google+ compared to other networks. More importantly, there are distinct differences in the way people use these networks. *Michael Steizner* of Social Media Examiner sums it up:

> *"Google Plus is more of an interest-based network, whereas Facebook is the place where people connect with others they already know."* **–Michael Steizner**

The Forrester on-line survey of 61,104 online U.S. adults was conducted in April 2013 and the results are reported in, "The Case for Google Plus". Nate Elliott, Vice President and principal analyst at Forrester writes:

---

* Words & phrases underlined (links) are cross-referenced with URL addresses at the back

"Google Plus can deliver bigger audiences and deeper engagement than you thing – and even offers marketers clear advantages over Twitter." –**Nate Elliott, Forrester**

Shareaholic looked at the data for the top 8 social media platforms in terms of visitor behavior and the report on "Social Referrals That Matter" is discussed in the next section.

Scoop #24: Links & SEO

Links on social networks are considered high-quality indicators by Google. Every time you share a link to your site, you build links for Google to index, which helps boost your ratings for SEO. Jennifer Barry's advice at business2community.com is to post quality content and remain in good standing, so as to keep your site's ranking intact. Good posts *may* help you boost other sites but bad posts *will* lead to a penalty.

Jennifer Barry also states, "the more links your page has, the faster Google will index the page. Your social media accounts attached to your page will show more links to your site and other sites you might share." She reminds us that the more quality content you share, the more traffic you drive to your site, and the indexing is done more quickly when influencers share it too.

Scoop #25: Authority links for networks

Social media networks are becoming increasingly more interested in expert content and authority link building helps with search rank. Google retired their authorship program (which gave authors added visibility with snippets in search results) but they continue to measure author rank for search results. +Rick Bucich wrote, "Authorship (the markup) is dead but Google attempting to measure authority via algorithm is not. In that sense it's business as usual; concentrate on building an audience and be seen as a topical expert."

Jennifer Barry makes this point at business2community.com. She says, "Again, there's nothing Google likes more than quality content. By linking any content you write to your Google+ account, you not only tell Google that a real person with actual experience with the subject matter wrote the blog, but you also tell readers that, too. Building trust is one of the most important aspects of content marketing, and you do that by establishing yourself as an expert in your field. Visitors will seek out your site to read information from an expert."

Facebook is following Google's lead and getting into authorship. They are boosting their Instant Article function to make it easy for Facebook readers to start following the author of an article they just read. They want publishers to use the Author Tag to grow their audiences. This is a web development tool that connects the byline in a story preview in the News Feed to the writer's Page or Profile with Follow. Facebook wants to keep audiences on their social network longer rather than click-off to other sites. Andrew Hutchinson writes:

"while it makes sense to publish direct to Facebook and have them assist you with reach, you're also supplanting your own website for the sake of Facebook's, and thus, building reliance on rented land… no one's going to give up their own website, a place they can monetize and control if they're not getting anything significant in return. And while Facebook is the number one driver of referral traffic on the web, it still needs to ensure that those who do publish on Facebook see that they will get results better than they could get by sticking with their current publishing process…" **– Andrew Hutchinson**

---

* Words & phrases underlined (links) are cross-referenced with URL addresses at the back

That's why Facebook is now measuring <u>time spent reading</u>. Their algorithm looks at the amount of time each reader takes to go through an article as an indicator of interest and uses it to show them more Instant Articles content. Author Tags boost the draw of Instant Articles and the ability to follow your favorite author and get notifications of their content on Facebook. That way Facebook will keep feeding users more directly posted content. "You might not want all of a certain publication, but you really like the way a certain author writes – now Facebook has a way to give you that content."

Scoop #26: Authority links for your domain

Authority links for your domain can help build a strong brand presence on the web, earn trust from your target audience, and connect to people with influence. <u>Venchito Tampon</u> explains that authority-link building is essential for small brands to establish influence within their niche and helps bigger brands stay ahead of competitors. Considering that the authority links for the referred domain are in its' niche, and qualified based on domain metrics (DA, PA, search share, Alexa) and brand metrics (social shares, readership, community strength), brands can benefit in many ways:

- Increased brand exposure to a wider audience targeted by the link sources
- Helps with conversions
- Passes authority to the linked domain
- Sends referred targeted visitors
- Gains social followers, readers, and brand loyalists

There are two types of authority links: absolute and relative. *Absolute* are backlinks from domains that have established authority and trust in different market segments (e.g. newspapers, television, and radio). *Relative* are backlinks from domains that have authority in a specific niche and high search share in their particular market segments. While both types of authority links can boost your domain ranking, relative authority links can pass converted visitors to your website in a specific market niche.

How to get authority links to your domain?

1. Produce link-bait content pieces
2. Invite authoritative guest authors
3. Ethical link reciprocation
4. Buy links ethically

You can build authority links by publishing link-bait pieces related to your market niche. Start on your own blog with one article per month that is tailored to a specific market segment and then progress to other segments that you want to establish authority in. You want to rank high in search for certain popular keywords. I put it to you this way: "you have to own the keywords".

Next, you want to approach other relevant domains:

1. Find a content gap on the website that you want to backlink from or better still, see if you can improve or turn some of their content into a linkable asset.
2. Help them create a linkable asset such as an infographic and guide.
3. Promote the content by posting it on industry forums and popular newsletters.
4. Once the buzz dies down, follow up with an email outreach campaign.

---

* Words & phrases underlined (links) are cross-referenced with URL addresses at the back

To establish authority links you have to keep publishing content that is original and unique consistently and often. And that takes resources which you may not have. That's where you invite authoritative guest authors to contribute. You can also build alliances with key influencers and active participants in your industry or buy links.

Scoop #27: Backlinks & hyperlinks – yah or nay?

Backlinks have become a topic of conversation lately. It's rumored that Google is doing away with them but my reading says they're still in vogue. What are backlinks? Ayesta Anwar's blog, "8 Most Constructive Ways to Build High Quality Backlinks" at bloggermentor.com, explains that backlinks are an incoming hyperlink that links a web page to another website's webpage, also referred to as authority links.

> *"Links are still the best way that we've found to discover [how relevant or important somebody is], and maybe over time social or authorship or other types of markup will give us a lot more information about that."* – **Matt Cutts, Google**

Backlinks can give content high ranks on search engines. The more backlinks the higher the PageRank but quality backlinks are far better than scrappy ones. To get high-quality backlinks requires effort. Anwar suggests these ways to build them:

1. Comment on other people's blogs – simple to do but you have to leave a quality and relevant comment that impresses other people enough to visit your blog.
2. Guest posting – find a recognized blog and submit one of your blogs for posting. You have to develop a relationship

with their author beforehand. Also keep posting regularly for results.

3. Become active on forums – join forums and engage, and this can build quality backlinks. By sharing you also increase your circle of bloggers and people in your profession.

4. Interview – build a professional relationship with popular bloggers and you may get an opportunity to ask them for an interview. When you consistently leave comments, share, and re-tweet their stuff, they'll start noticing you.

5. Create videos – uploading videos to YouTube will help you get quality backlinks. Video tutorials are quite popular, for example, how to start a new blog or how to upload a video, etc.

6. Long posts with images and charts – create quality posts which are helpful and instructive. Write how-to posts and that will get people visiting your blog.

7. Write e-books – write an e-book on a topic that appeals to you and your audience, and get people to share it. Submit it to top social marketing websites.

8. Offer products for free on your blog – free is a keyword that people investigate. Offer free services like e-books or templates, even if you have to buy it yourself.

"The philosophy that we've always had is if you make something that's compelling then it would be much easier to get people to write about it and to link to it. Make a fantastic website that people love and tell their friends about and link to and want to experience. As a result, your website starts to become stronger and stronger in the rankings." – **Matt Cutts, Google**

---

* Words & phrases underlined (links) are cross-referenced with URL addresses at the back

Scoop #28: Social bookmarking sites

Social bookmarking sites are like networking sites, where users share links. When you use sites like StumbleUpon, Digg, Delicious, and Technorati, you permit them to add your links into their sites or marketing lists. This is how your URLs can go viral and get more exposure. But your links have to be on "DoFollow" to create quality backlinks. "NoFollow" backlinks are not as good and don't help you get high PageRank. This scoop is from a blog by Ayesha Anwar, "50 DoFollow Social Bookmarking Sites to Get DoFollow Backlinks" at bloggermentor.com.

Scoop #29: Off-page SEO

Off-page SEO can help speed up the link-building process and boost search ranking to get you more website traffic. But off-page SEO involves more than link building. Brand signals, co-citations and latent semantic indexing are among the concepts that have to be understood to get the link building strategy implemented according to Venchito Tampon. There are 11 strategies discussed in his blog:

1. Use latent semantic indexing (LSI) keywords as link phrases (improves a page's relevance to a specific search query) to help Google understand the page by looking at synonyms and connecting keywords / phrases.

    The contents of a webpage are crawled by a search engine and the most common words and phrases are collated and identified as the keywords for the page. LSI looks for synonyms related to the title of your page. For example, if the title of your page was "Classic Cars", the search engine would expect to find words relating to that subject in the content of the page as well, i.e. "collectors", "automobile", "Bentley", "Austin" and "car auctions". (Source: http://www.searchenginejournal.com/what-is-latent-semantic-indexing-seo-defined/21642/)

2. Convert highly useful PDFs to accessible pages – find three or four papers related to your industry, compile all information into one page (make sure all details are interrelated with each other), then publish it on your blog.

3. Improve relevance with keyword integration to brand – help search engines understand what your brand is all about and the purpose of each of your pages – brand recall should be evident.

4. Create targeted landing pages for external web properties to increase click through.

5. Boost social following with Manage Flitter – <u>Social signals</u> are off-site SEO signals that strongly indicate a site's user activity or behavior and can help its page(s) rank higher in search results with a minimum requirement for links.

6. Build authentic and personal relationships with people in the industry.

7. Get cited links from supplier websites – getting backlinks from general supplier sites would help customers to directly find your brand. For example, create a profile in <u>Thomasnet,</u> add a link pointing to your company site, complete all the information and earn some referral traffic once your page has been published.

8. Identify ranking potential through link analysis – one way of determining if there's a ranking potential in a particular keyword or set of keywords is by looking at the average number of referring domains for each page listed in search engine result pages (SERPs).

9. Acquire image links by inviting guest contributors – to keep up the frequency of blogging; this can also help acquire authoritative backlinks.

10. Move the ladder by pointing out specific pages for broken links – when you collect all the data such as broken URLs

---

* Words & phrases underlined (links) are cross-referenced with URL addresses at the back

and anchor texts, try to understand why these links are broken. Search for the correct links and include them to your outreach.

11. Use Launchrock to build trust signals for new websites – it is a site builder platform that can help you create one landing page (it may be the homepage) for your website.

Scoop #30: Social factors critical to search rank

"Search engine ranking is all about social" is how Jason Barret titles his blog. The byline is "Before it was important, now it's critical." He points out that Google has invested massively in their SEO algorithm and search capabilities, and their biggest focus is content quality. Barret explains that in the past links improved search rank based on the premise that good content gets shared, but that was a one-trick pony that got exploited and Google caught on. There's a lot more to it now and social tops the list.

Anyone trying to keep up with Google would find it challenging. They are forever changing and adding apps and features. So what social features has Google been working on lately?

1. There was a lot of speculation on community boards about how Google+ posts get ranked in terms of likes (+1s) and shares, for example.
2. People wondered if Google+ brand pages ranked higher than Facebook pages or Twitter profiles (see Scoop #71)
3. Barret says that Google takes issue with social network developers restricting content from Google search results.
4. Google search has been working on answering questions directly in search. What about people who jump at the chance to answer questions? For now search shows both.

5. Review Extension allows people to include one-line <u>reviews</u> in the AdWords that companies were paying for.

> "<u>Review extensions</u> allow advertisers to enrich their search ads by adding a line of text that highlights an award or 3rd party certification, such as Google Trusted Stores status. <u>Learn more</u> about review extensions."

How does social and search figure into all this? Searchmetrics Data produced a chart showing how social, backlinks, *onpage* (technical) and *onpage* (content) correlate with Google search.

Barret points out that seven out of the top eight factors affecting natural search are all social: Google +1, Facebook shares, Facebook total, Facebook comments, Facebook likes, Pinterest, and Tweets. Number of backlinks sneaks into third spot. What this tells you is that it's not enough to set up a Google Profile, Facebook Page or Pinterest board. Google measures continuous engagement in terms of comments, likes, shares, and Google +1s. Other social factors include: position of keyword in title, word count, keywords in body, keyword in external links, image count, and video integration. By studying the chart, you'll get an idea of what your focus should be in your social media strategy.

All this makes your social and SEO easier if you consider them both in your marketing practices:

- Track conversions – look at social and website together
- Storytelling – your social profiles and posts should be telling the same story as your website
- Key Performance Indicators (KPI's) – Social, SEO, and digital tasks should be part of a holistic approach. People assigned to both tasks should be collaborating on the same goals and measuring the same KPI's

---

* Words & phrases underlined (links) are cross-referenced with URL addresses at the back

Barret adds that collaboration can be hard. New systems may be needed and it may require more resources. He recommends looking at Huddle or Box, and thinking about the content that's being produced and how to tell the story in different ways with your mixture of social channels. "Each social network has its own nuances around etiquette, messaging and general use. Each team needs to be an equal partner in this new relationship."

In the end it comes down to leadership. Someone has to sign off on the plan. Chances are that people at the top don't know about meta tags (unless it's a digital business). Assign a leader to oversee the practice, set KPI's and agree on options.

It's important to get your social, SEO and content on the same page. Get a strategy with a clear set of goals and KPI's. Eric Schmidt, Google Chairman said that they underestimated social and won't make those mistakes again, so plan on growing your social practices.

Scoop #31: Local audiences & profiles

Don't forget your local audience. Add your geographic location on your social media profiles and pages if you want people in your local area to find you. Also, a lot of searches are done on mobile devices while people are travelling. Often Google knows where you want to go before you do. The establishments that get ranked highest on Google Search will most likely get that business. You may not have a lot of local competition but you won't necessarily be ranked highest if you don't have your location on your Profile. (The Local business Page can really help you with local audiences.)

Organic Reach & Followers

Scoop #32: Where to start

How and where do you share your content? The answer to this question is sprinkled throughout this book (e.g. scoop #69) but let's review some options:

1. Social media costs you the least for the most exposure and you can do so much with it — PR, advertising, surveys, contests, coupons, sales and so forth. +Warren Coakley suggests that you share your content on communities, Facebook, Twitter, LinkedIn, Xing, Vine, Instagram, and YouTube, and use hashtags to gain a wider audience.

   - Don't spread yourself out too thin. Pick a couple of networks where your target audience hangs out. Read what experts have to say about how to decide which network is best for you (e.g., scoops #22 and #23)
   - It's important that you engage with your followers routinely. If you drop in, post something that you want promoted and don't engage until the next round some time later, you won't get very far. Most social networks require that you establish yourself as part of that community and that takes time.

---

* Words & phrases underlined (links) are cross-referenced with URL addresses at the back

2. Build a website and/or blog – establishes your brand as permanent and gives it a URL address. Customers expect to see a website for brands they deal with. Most people do research on the web before deciding where to shop. And you'll benefit from organic search.

3. Syndication – use third-party sites to distribute your content (snippets, links, blog posts, web pages, videos). Any partnership you form can help you build awareness. They can have strict requirements too in terms of RSS feeds, custom-selected URLs, thumbnail images, titles, etc.

4. Video and slide presentations are an excellent way for you to pitch your content and drive traffic to your blog or website to gain leads. By posting informational content on YouTube and Slideshare for example, you can promote your content via links on social networks.

5. Large distributors like Amazon – digital and print, audio, games, software, etc.

6. Email your work colleagues and give them the links so they can share with their networks also.

7. Start an email campaign. Email suppliers, customers, and prospects. If you don't have an email list, start one. If your offer is compelling, subscribers will opt in. Remember to give people the option to unsubscribe.

8. Don't forget newsletters. They have a higher conversion rate than blogs, for example, and you can publish them online.

9. Old tactics still work especially for promotion locally. Submit feature stories and articles to local newspapers and magazines. Make flyers and drop them into your local stores and people's mailboxes. Snail mail has been mostly abandoned by business. I get only notices and bills. But that's the point – so few items are dropped in my mailbox that I notice every one. You can also place flyers in local

      libraries, restaurants, gyms, community centers, and other locations where your audience visits.

10. Radio and TV advertising – spot placement, sponsorship ads, commercials, and infomercials. More and more viewers consume their media on the internet but that just means that costs have come down on these channels while the potential to reach a mass audience remains.

11. Make presentations to local boards of trade, meetup groups and special events.

Don't forget that people have to see or hear your message about seven times before they pay attention. Don't give up.

Scoop #33: Facebook organic reach

It's no secret that Facebook posts have a low organic reach as a result of changes made to their algorithm. In a <u>sales deck</u> obtained by Ad Age in November 2013, Facebook told its partners that they expected organic distribution of an individual's page posts to gradually decline over time while they worked to improve the users' experience on the site. According to <u>Ogilvy released data</u> brand pages they manage reached only 6% of fans. For pages with more than 500,000 fans, Ogilvy said reach was only 2%. Needless to say, there was much discontent among marketers and agencies. Some were so upset by how often Facebook changed the rules they planned to focus more resources on other networks like Twitter and LinkedIn.

According to <u>Nate Elliott's blog</u>, Facebook was failing marketers. One advertiser referred to Facebook as "<u>one of the most lucrative grifts of all time</u>." Marketers also worried that many of their fans were fake, based on the fact that <u>many marketers</u> and <u>many publishers</u> reported that huge percentages of their fans were

---

* Words & phrases underlined (links) are cross-referenced with URL addresses at the back

from emerging markets where they did not expect to find an audience.

Has anything changed in the past year or so? A blog published by adwick.com in March 2015 says that Facebook's organic "reach is not quite dead". You decide if that's the case. A study by social analytics and Locowise conducted in February 2015, looked at 500 pages with 215,000 likes on 27,000 posts and found that:

- Average organic reach was 11% for pages with fewer than 10,0000 likes; 6% for pages with 10,000 to 99,000 likes; 5% for over 100,000 likes; and 7% of total likes
- Posts with links drew the most organic reach, at 18%; then videos at 9%; text-only status updates at 9%; and photos at 7%; links pushed organic reach to 32% for pages with fewer than 10,000 likes

Based on the study, Locowise suggested you should stop posting photos directly and include them as thumbnails in link posts instead. Posting more links also increases traffic to your website or blog and allows you to track the traffic from Facebook too.

They also found that videos, which weren't getting much reach two months before, are getting higher ranking. They suggest you upload videos from your YouTube channel directly onto Facebook and create more video content to improve organic reach.

Scoop #34: Facebook organic-reach growth

Reports on organic-reach growth for Facebook Pages after making changes to their algorithm, showed that marketers also used advertising. A study of 1,000 pages by social media analytics tool Locowise shows that on average, organic reach went up by 6% in December 2013 compared to November. Only 38% of the Pages reported an increase in organic reach that month, which means that 62% saw a decrease. Pages with fan bases between 257 fans and 50 million fans were chosen randomly for the study, and included consumer packaged goods, car manufacturers, sports and music celebrities, B2B, B2C, and small business. The result may also be skewed by the fact that paid reach rose in December, as 25 percent more marketers chose to advertise posts. Of the 1,000 pages analyzed, 41 percent used paid media but viral reach was down 3%. Some 53% of the pages showing increases in organic reach also boosted some posts.

Scoop #35: Social media post-click engagement

How engaged are the visitors on your favorite social networks? Given the amount of time we spend on social media sharing and interacting with posts, you may be wondering how everyone else behaves post click. Which social network do you think drives the most engaged referrals? Shareaholic looked at average visit duration, pages per visit, and bounce rate for visitors referred to their network from the top 8 social media platforms and reported the results in "Social Referrals That Matter".

Their chart of Social Media Post-Click Engagement discussed by Danny Wong is based on data from average activity across 200,000 sites reaching 250+ million unique visitors monthly over six months. Shareaholic looked at data from YouTube, Google+, LinkedIn, Twitter, Facebook, Pinterest, Reddit, and StumpleUpon:

1. Not surprisingly, YouTube steals the show. That site drives the most engaged traffic and has the lowest average bounce rate (43.19%), the highest pages per visit (2.99) and the longest average time (227.82 seconds).

* Words & phrases underlined (links) are cross-referenced with URL addresses at the back

2. Google+ and LinkedIn drive the fewest social referrals but deliver the best visitors. On average Google+ users spend more than 3 minutes diving into shared posts and connecting. They visit 2.45 pages during each visit and the bounce rate is 50.63%. LinkedIn users spend about 2 minutes and 13 seconds on each link they click and view 2.23 pages on each visit. Their bounce rate is 51.28%. You may consider investing time on these networks even with minimal referral traffic from these sites.

3. Twitter and Facebook are tied in 4th place – referral from Twitter is as good as Facebook's in terms of bounce rate (56.35%). Twitter gets more pages per visit (2.15 vs. 2.03) and Facebook spend more time on a site post-click than Twitter users (127.44 seconds vs. 123.10).

4. Pinterest is 6th and pinners bounce as often as Facebook and Twitter users but view fewer pages per visit (1.71) and spend a lot less time on the site (64.67 seconds), slightly better than StumbleUpon.

5. Reddit have a high bounce rate (70.16%) and visitors are hard to please – very selective about content that gets upvoted and eager to downvote when they disagree.

6. StumbleUpon drives the least engaged referrals. Post-click, on average users view only 1.5 pages per visit and spend 54.09 seconds on the site. They also are quick to "like" or "dislike".

While Facebook's organic reach is diminishing and frustrating visitors, YouTube has just released a new Creator playbook for brands. However, it should be stated that your overall goal should be to engage people. That means your focus must be to produce the best content – quality will get you the shares.

Scoop #36: Social media commitment

Engagement is about building relationships and that requires work. You have to read the posts, comment, like (+1), and share. And it's not a one-time thing. Relationships are built over time by people who show consistency. You can't just create an account or post something and then ignore it. Your followers have to know they can rely on you. There's reciprocity involved. You not only have to respond to mentions and comments, it's important that you also mention others and "add your own comments". This type of engagement will help share opinions of you and your brand.

Scoop #37: Social media spam

Followers will not stay with you for long if all you do is spew out marketing and sales pitches in your posts. When this happens people come to see you as a spammer and will ignore your posts. To avoid falling into this trap, I recommend applying the 80:20 rule to your activity on networks. This split ratio of social to promotional sharing gets the job done without annoying people. Eighty percent of the time, you should be sharing content that is helpful and supportive without expecting anything in return.

Scoop #38: The influence of followers

It is important to have good followers in your social media networks. They can be advocates for your brand and often share their opinions with their supporters. According to Jennifer Barry at *business2community.com,* research indicates that 92% of consumers trust recommendations from friends, family, and other reliable sources. Often consumer preferences are based on what

* Words & phrases underlined (links) are cross-referenced with URL addresses at the back

they've heard on social media. She points out that the opposite is also true. This is why she recommends not buying Twitter followers, spamming LinkedIn connections, or creating bogus accounts for more shares, which hurt you in the long run.

Scoop #39: Testimonials on your website

People really want to know what others think. That's a tip that you can use to create content that works for you. Use your social media posts to share recommendations, reviews, testimonials, and positive comments about your products and services. Think of your post as a mini-landing page which can drive traffic to your website. When someone searches for a product you are carrying, they may end up on your Google+ page and that in turn can direct them to your website. Jennifer Barry at *business2community.com* says that while third-party sources may carry the reviews, customers prefer hearing what others say about your brand from you. This is a good way to boost traffic to your website.

Scoop #40: Keywords for more followers

Keywords are another way of reaching out to Followers that are not presently in your circles. Use the keyword(s) to add important phrases that someone might be entering in Google Search. To come up with the best keyword(s) or keyword phrases, consider how someone would search for your product. Jennifer Barry at *business2community.com* gives another important tip, "Make sure the most important search terms show up in your profiles for your social media accounts". Use your top keywords in the most important places on your social media pages, like the heading, and the opening and closing lines of your text, for example.

Scoop #41: Hashtags – laser beams

Hashtags are a variation on keywords – the laser beam version. Hashtags are used to identify messages on specific topics and grab the attention of people interested in that topic. When you add hashtags to your post, you cast a wider net for engagement and scoop up followers. Hashtags always begin with the hash or pound sign (#) and follow with one word or a phrase that misses all the spaces, for example #soogood or #trendingtopics. Google+ adds hashtags automatically to posts when the Profile or Page settings allow it. You can make up your own hashtags and get people to adopt them. If the hashtags you're using fit the message and the content is good, people will adopt them. Hashtags are also a great way of tagging your posts so you can track them easily and monitor performance.

Scoop #42: How to use hashtags

Lynn Serfinn's blog at *the7gracesofmarketing.com* about "The 7 Graces of Marketing – Ethical Marketing for Social Entrepreneurs" explains how to use hashtags on Twitter or Facebook:

- Use hashtags on trending topics or news that is current to engage more people and reach a wider audience. The hashtags should be relevant to your post.
- Use hashtags to find people of interest to you, like influencers.
- Make up a unique hashtag to create brand awareness. Use the same hashtag on related posts to see how a campaign

---

* Words & phrases underlined (links) are cross-referenced with URL addresses at the back

is going. If you link your post to your website or blog, you may get migration as well.

Scoop #43: Do's & don'ts of hashtags

The right hashtags can broaden your audience and encourage them to share your content. How do you pick the right hashtags for your post? Rick Ramos of Rick Ramos Consulting, shared a post with an infographic on "How to use hashtags on Google+ (infographic)" at *+Rick Ramos*. I've used some of his do's and don'ts for my infographic:

First the do's:

- ✓ Do pair your hashtags with images – it's a great way of boosting views
- ✓ Do aim to use 2 to 3 hashtags per post – more than one is great but too many is distracting
- ✓ Do include Hashtags when you post to communities – it's the best way to foster engagement and track conversations
- ✓ Do take advantage of trending hashtags that relate to your content – it's a great way to add followers
- ✓ Do run hashtag-related campaigns and track metrics related to those campaigns – by using hashtags with advertising on newspapers, radio, and TV, for example, you can track on-line response and brand engagement

Now for the don'ts:

- ▪ Don't try to replace quality posts with hashtags – hashtags can't substitute for content and that puts people off
- ▪ Don't hashtag every word in your post – remember that 2 is a party but 3 is a crowd

- Don't use very long hashtags that are hard to read – people skip them altogether
- Don't use trending hashtags without knowing why they are trending – make sure it's a topic you associate with
- Don't use hashtags for trending topics that have nothing to do with your post – readers will avoid your posts

---

Scoop #44: Engagement versus content type

It is reasonable to assume that different types of content get different amounts of engagement. I wanted a comparison and reviewed a couple of blogs that reported on what some pros were doing. The New York Times creates different content for engagement versus clicks. They admit they haven't been doing it right in the past but have learned from their Innovation Report that you have to plan for both content creation and distribution. Their staff writer Jenna Wortham has been on social media for a while and likes it. She had to learn how to combine both personal and professional messages in her strategy. You can't just bombard people with irrelevant content. Instead "you can use Twitter, Instagram, Vine like your online calling card". You can't just tweet, "read this, read this, read this".

Alex MacCallum, assistant managing editor of audience development, says that they use certain strategies at The Times to drive traffic versus engagement. On Facebook they'll post a core nugget of a story with a beautiful visual. On Twitter, they'll use a Twitter card that gives the "crux of the story". For example, for the Paris attacks they created social assets for "here's what we know, and here's what we don't know" and included three bullets for each.

They've seen a correlation between the number of people that engage with The Times on social media and the number of fans. MacCallum said they would be launching an Instagram account focused on visual storytelling. They've looked at what National Geographic is doing on Instagram and like it because it made them relevant for a young audience.

NewsWhip analyzed how "Different Types Of Content Attract Different Facebook Interaction". They looked at different type of engagement in January on posts from five different kinds of content publishers:

1. Bleacher Report for sports
2. Politico for political news
3. The Atlantic for long-form articles
4. TMZ for celebrity news
5. PlayBuzz for interactive quizzes

What did they learn about interactions for different content type? They report that generally likes and comments are a brilliant way to extend the reach of a story and other content such as videos, across News Feeds. It's how Facebook surfaces content and puts it in front of more eyeballs.

1. Sports stories get a very high *Like* ratio, presumably as a quick nod. When "a supporter sees a headline like 'New England Patriots Win Super Bowl', they *Like* the post without clicking through. They know their team won the game, but they want to acknowledge it to their friends on Facebook." They also get a lot of likes through Spike from stories that name big sports stars in their title, similarly to celebrity sites".
   They postulate that in stories where there's a clear outcome, like a match report or celebrity news or even

breaking news events, the reader is more likely to acknowledge the story with a *Like* and not click through and read it. Hence, the headline with any excerpt delivers enough of a preview in their News Feed, and is crucial. While they may scan through the comments, they'll hesitate to click on a link unless absolutely necessary, especially on mobile.

2. The engagement is different for political content. This type of content gets a decent <u>comment</u> ratio. Many U.S. political blogs get high rankings on Facebook and Politico, and also attract a high ratio of comments (31%). People have strong opinions and like to debate them.

3. Long-form articles can also generate a lot of comments and discussion. When an article addresses a current important issue, people take the time to read it and are more likely to share their thoughts. This is good news for publishers wondering if they should invest the time.

4. Interactives and lists are really popular on Facebook and "clock up big shares, especially if they're personalized". The content is opposite to long form articles but the appeal is just as strong. PlayBuzz's interactive quizzes on Facebook offer proof of strong engagement. Another example is "<u>BuzzFeed</u>'s lists of the 31 reasons why you know you're from Ontario". Why does this type of content go viral? Because the reader can relate to it, talk and laugh about it.

On any social network and with any type of content, shares are the best indicator for social engagement. NewsWhip sums it up this way, "Ultimately, <u>shares</u> remain the No. 1 indicator of social engagement with a story for many publishers. They indicate a

---

* Words & phrases underlined (links) are cross-referenced with URL addresses at the back

clear expression of interest in a story, and are given preferential treatment by Facebook's <u>algorithm</u>".

Get more expert advice on this topic in Scoop #78 – Content Stream.

Scoop #45: Psychology of engagement

We spend a lot of time on social media. Why the obsession? QuickSprout created an infographic that can help us learn more about why people use Facebook. The data can help us deliver content that satisfies the need on any network. <u>Why we like, share, comment on Facebook</u> illustrates that fundamentally Facebook taps the brain's pleasure center. Research shows psychological reactions like pupil dilation as an indication of happiness when people are browsing their Facebook.

Why do we click on "Like"? According to Facebook, it's a way to give positive feedback or to connect with things we care about. (Research shows on average 44% Like content once daily and 29% do it more often.) Specifically, these reasons are given:

1. It's a quick and easy nod
2. To affirm something about ourselves – a study of more than 58,000 people revealed that we can tell a lot about the person. Are they white or African American? Gay or straight? Democrat or Republican? Male of female? Age?
3. To express virtual empathy – spending more time on social networks and engaging in instant message chats was found to be a predictor of virtual empathy.
4. Because it's practical and we get something back from favorite brands, such as coupons and updates

Why we comment? Because we feel we have something to say and it's more satisfying to comment or receive comments rather than Likes. That was confirmed in a study of 1,200 Facebook users.

Why do we post Status Updates? The stats say that people update their status on Facebook daily (10%), several times per day (4%), or never (25%). Posting relieves loneliness – research showed that when students updated their Facebook status more often, they reported lower levels of loneliness.

What stops us from posting? Self-censorship – we stop ourselves. Research indicated that 71% of users type out at least one status or comment and don't post it. Users changed their minds about 5.52 statuses and 3.2 comments.

Why do we Share? A worldwide poll by Ipsos showed that: 61% share interesting things; 43% share important things; 43% share funny things; 37% share what they believe in and who they really are; 30% recommend a product service, movie, book, etc.; 29% add their support to a cause, an organization, a belief, etc.; 26% share unique things; 22% want others to know what they're doing; 20% add to a thread or conversation; and 10% show they're in the know.

Get more expert advice on this topic in Scoop #81 – Content that sells.

Scoop #46: Social media contests

Contests are another way to increase engagement. Jennifer Barry at *business2community.com* suggests that social media contests can arouse the interest of followers who were only familiar with the brand in passing. A good contest can create a buzz and bring

* Words & phrases underlined (links) are cross-referenced with URL addresses at the back

people out of the woodwork. To make the most of the new traffic, be sure to direct them to your website (link). Social media posts can be a great way of announcing a contest.

Scoop #47: Daily routine

Follow a daily routine that helps you create social interactions with your followers. Daniel Sharkov's blog at reviewzntips.com, "5 Steps Google Plus Checklist to Help You Create more Interactions", will help you make connections and add followers.

1. Re-share an article you found helpful. Similarly to a retweet, the post is shared on your timeline, with credit going to the originator. Share something at least once a day.

2. Share a funny post and give credit. Some of the most popular content in social media has humor. Vines and memes are very popular. Make sure it has some relevance to your niche and your followers' interests. Save the images in an archive to reuse when you need something in a hurry.

3. To get more engagement, create a post from a page in your blog. Don't just paste a link. You need to upload an image rather than leave the link thumbnail image. Type some text for emphasis. Use hashtags and then post it daily.

4. Find and follow at least 10 people every day. You'll find new content and interesting people, who will probably add you to their circles.

5. Engage in social media. Leave at least one comment per day. That will get you noticed and shows your expertise. Thank people for their comments. Answer questions.

You may be interested in hearing about my routine. I try to post throughout the day. I share what I've found online that I think is useful to my followers. I share original content and occasionally I promote my books or videos. Most of the time, I share other people's posts. My supporters are very good about sharing my posts, so the rule of reciprocity works quite well for me. My credo is:

✓ Be useful
✓ Be authentic
✓ Sell a little

I am most active on Twitter at this time but I used to be more active on Google+ before. In order to keep my posts "fresh" and keep me organized, I have numerous buckets of posts to pick from throughout the day. The labels on my buckets are as follows:

- Business & Product promotion
- Website & Blog content
- Humor / Questions / Puzzles / Teasers
- Motivational & Inspirational quotes
- Business & Social Media tips
- Community & Causes
- Personal sharing

Consider these ideas and come up with a routine that works for you.

Scoop #48: Best time to post

Everyone wants to know the best time to post on social networks. BufferSocial analyzed over 4.8 million tweets across 10,000 of

---

* Words & phrases underlined (links) are cross-referenced with URL addresses at the back

their user profiles to find the best time to tweet. They looked at how clicks and engagement and timing occur throughout the day and in different time zones. This is what they found:

- Early mornings are the best time to tweet in order to get clicks
- Evenings and late at night are the best time, on average, for total engagement with your tweets
- In some cases, the most popular times to post are opposite of the best times to post
- Popular times and best times to tweet differ across time zones

Lee Smallwood's blog, "What are the Best Times to Post on Google+" at *snaphix.com,* shows that there is no one time that is best for everyone. We can assume that the same behavioral science applies to all social networks. Lee presents data sets for four trending #hashtags on "Explore Google+" collected using NOD3X saved projects, and concludes that there is no generic best time to post on Google+. He explains that you cannot expect people interested in photography to be posting on exactly the same day and the same time as people who like music. For example, for #artanddesign, the data results showed Tuesday, Monday, and Friday at 6 am, 3 pm, and 1 pm had the most engagement, and the optimum was Tuesday at 6 am. For #automotive, the data results showed Monday, Wednesday, and Tuesday at 2 pm, 3pm, and 9pm had the most engagement and the optimum was Monday at 2 pm. As an added tip, Lee suggests you can use NOD3X to track certain #hashtags for your projects.

Scoop #49: Advanced socialbots on Twitter

The article "How Advanced Socialbots Have Infiltrated Twitter", which was shared by +Eli Fennel at technologyreview.com reports on studies done by Carlos Freitas at the Federal University of Minas Gerais in Brazil and a few of his pals. Their work reveals that socialbots have infiltrated the Twitter platform and it has become hard to distinguish them from real users. With advances in artificial intelligence, these sophisticated socialbots can have real influence on the network. That's because a tweet is limited to a 140 character string, which forces people to write in broken syllables. Add hashtags and handles, and you have mashed-up language. We have become used to reading shorthand. This mashed-up language can be simulated by Socialbots fairly well and twitter is unable to detect these over two-thirds of these bot accounts, according to Freitas.

Freitas et al followed three groups of humans: Group 1: 200 random people from twitter stream; Group 2: 200 people who post regularly about software; Group 3: 200 sofware developers who were socially connected on twitter. The Klout score is an online service that measures the influence of Twitter accounts, giving them a score between 0 and 100, and Freitas found socialbots achieved Klout scores of the same order as several academicians and social network researchers.

---

* Words & phrases underlined (links) are cross-referenced with URL addresses at the back

Sales & Marketing

Scoop #50: Sales acceleration

Sales acceleration is what everyone wants for their business. But what exactly does that involve? Ken Krogue lists "27 Sales Acceleration Principles and Best Practices" at forbes.com. It's a great digest for this section that covers the essential points. I've also created a neat keyboard infographic so you can view them at a glance:

1. Sell remotely – that's how professional selling is now done. The phone and the web make face-to-face sales a thing of the past. The hybrid model combines inside sales with outside sales.
2. Specialize – think of Henry Ford and the assembly line. Split off before-sales from after-sales groups. Then split appointment setters and closers. Also split by size of account and vertical market. Use Moneyball tactics from *blogs.salesforce.com*
3. Strategize – get a clear strategy for each element of sales and marketing (leads, lists, offers, and skill of salespeople).
4. Define process – watch, analyze, and design the best process for sales and marketing.
5. Test – test between two options to find the best way (A/B split testing).

6. Optimize – continually test and evaluate variables to improve the process and the outcome.

7. Align – align all the elements and get everyone and everything on the same page.

8. Qualify – Use ANUM – who are the people with the *authority* to buy? Do they have a *need* for what you offer? The greater the need, the more *urgency* and *money* appear.

9. Profile – find qualified companies and people; validate contact data and sales intelligence, which will help engagement.

10. Map – map out market fit between companies and organizational structure to help you navigate need and decision-making process that moves the sale forward towards closure.

11. Educate – create awareness of what your business offers through PR and marketing, which moves interest into need. This is where content marketing strategies come in. Give your prospects the information they need about your industry, company, and product so they move from awareness *to* curiosity *to* interest *to* need.

12. Bridge media – move from passive marketing media like brand advertising, radio, print, or email to active media like web response, social media, phone calls, and finally face-to-face. Research shows that LinkedIn messages, for example, improve response ratios by 700% over same message by email.

13. Power tools – use the right tools for sales acceleration, such as cloud-based CRM software like Salesforce.com, contract profiling like LinkedIn, and power dialer technology.

---

* Words & phrases underlined (links) are cross-referenced with URL addresses at the back

14. Inbound marketing – Marketing is about getting the leads. A lead comes to you with a need. A list is a record that can help you generate leads.

15. Response management – the process of responding immediately, persistently, and with other best practices to improve the odds of contacting and qualifying inbound marketing leads.

16. Immediacy – do it now and do it fast. Research shows the average company takes over 39 hours to initiate a response on a web-generated lead. Often leads are dropped.

17. Persistency – people want to talk to you but are very busy. Best practice is between 6 and 9 calls and 2-3 emails and voicemail.

18. Collaborate – join with other companies and people that don't compete to target the same prospects and customers.

19. Calibrate – make sure everyone is watching the same thing at the same time.

20. Measure – watch leading indicators, which are measurements that indicate what is about to happen.

21. Score – sales is getting the leads and scoring the goal – making the sale.

22. Gamify – make work fun; apply sports rules to work environments.

23. Predict – big data analytics which looks at lead sources, offer types, salesperson skill sets, and even weather patterns, stock market variations, and lunar cycles allow one to predict outcomes of sales and marketing interactions.

24. Visualize – need real-time data to make changes and win. Salespeople have to see progress in a simple display,

managers need to see rates and ratios, and executives need to see trends and ROI to make wise decisions.

25. Avoid decay – the downside of specialization is decay and delay; every handoff can lead to a breakdown in communication.

26. Lessen delay – sales acceleration constantly measures time and lessens delay.

27. Systemize – put all the best practices into a system which gets automated and continuously improved. Work it out manually; next put it on paper; then automate it like in a spreadsheet; when it works automate and pull it together into a system.

Scoop #51: Social selling

When it comes to social networking, I think we would all agree that the more people spread the word the better. According to Ken Krouge's blog at forbes.com, "Social Selling: 1 Big Idea to be 38x More Effective", businesses could be using their employees to share on social networks on behalf of their companies. Employee advocacy, as it's called, is part of the new sales segment: Sales Acceleration. Ken says that businesses have been too focused on the risks from information leakages and gaffes, and misuse of social media on the job. The rewards far outweigh the risks. By training and inviting employees to support sales efforts, you get a "veritable communications and social selling engine". This is exactly what you're hoping to get from loyal customers, advisers, and partners, so why not inside people?

In what areas could your employees support your business? Chris Boudreaux and Susan F. Emerick are experts on Sales

---

* Words & phrases underlined (links) are cross-referenced with URL addresses at the back

Acceleration. In their book, "The Most Powerful Brand on Earth" they list four areas:

1. Awareness – share information on the industry and your brand
2. Campaigns – spread the word about contests and offers, and get people excited
3. Support – your experts can educate your audience. Not only do they gain authority but their expertise can reflect positively on your brand
4. Talent – they can help you recruit people, with the right skillset, that fit into the organization's culture

Research by *everyonesocial.com* looked at the degree of sharing when you attach a link to Facebook or Twitter in an email message, versus allowing employees to share directly on social networks. They found messages were shared 38 times more frequently on a platform that makes it easy to share. According to the Chief Revenue Officer at *kitedesk.com*, by leveraging the network of the average employees, you can tap into an additional 2,500 people.

Scoop #52: Inbound versus outbound marketing

Marketing terminology has changed recently because the way we do marketing nowadays is different. In my opinion, if it's good marketing, then it doesn't feel like marketing, and what you call it won't matter. But some familiarity with the terms can lead to a better understanding of the practices. Since there is overlap, it's hard to split topics and treat them separately. You'll find some topics covered in this section would fit just as well in the next or vice versa. But let's get into the terminology. "Content marketing" is the new catchphrase and the new way of making a splash in the social media stream. (The next section is all about content marketing.) The other catchphrases are "inbound marketing" and "marketing automation". What's the distinction and does it matter? Marketers generally agree that content marketing is a subset of inbound marketing.

Inbound marketing is just one step in the buying cycle. Inbound marketing fills the top of your marketing funnel with leads while marketing automation nurtures and converts them into business.

Generally, the best strategy is to have a combination of inbound and outbound marketing. Your inbound marketing will attract people to your content and engage them, hopefully driving them to a form on a landing page that captures their data. Then your outbound marketing takes over and nurtures the leads with messaging relevant to their stage in the buying cycle. If you have a sales team, outbound marketing would support them as they become involved in the purchase decision right through to closing the business transaction.

Inbound marketing is about attracting visitors to your website and directing them to different places and offers from there. It requires creating content that helps you get found via SEO and social media. Your inbound marketing content includes your website, blog, white papers, videos, posts and landing pages.

Your inbound marketing practices include your content assets but are not limited to them. Without content you can't attract anybody. But without inbound projects – like technical SEO, authority links, freemium trials, interactive tools – that may be outside of the content marketer's scope, your marketing engine will stall. You have to use all the inbound practices or you'll limit the potential impact of your campaigns.

* Words & phrases underlined (links) are cross-referenced with URL addresses at the back

Traditionally, we focused on "outbound marketing" with outreach practices like telemarketing, mass mailers, newsletters, advertising, sales calls, trade shows, etc. But the internet has flipped the process around and there is more focus now on "inbound marketing", which has to abide by the rules of "permission marketing".

Outbound marketing continues to use mass advertising (TV, radio, magazines, billboards) and phone calls to send messages out, but has been augmented with targeted advertising (PPC, remarketing) and emails.

Marketing automation relies on software and databases to support inbound and outbound marketing practices.

When a visitor comes to your website, software tracks what they are interested in by monitoring the pages they visit, where they click on the page, and what they download. It monitors what the visitor is interested in. Once you capture the visitor's email address they become a lead. The marketing automation software uses the Customer Relationship Management (CRM) database to send emails and offers that nurture the lead's interests and needs. Depending on the content they consume, you can also determine where that lead is in terms of the buying cycle. Once they become a prospect, a sales person can follow up. (Source)

Scoop #53: SEO versus PPC

Search Engine Optimization (SEO) has to be part of your overall marketing strategy if you want people to find your website. Even if Google changes its search algorithm a couple hundred times a year, it should not affect your website ranking as long as

Webmaster Guidelines are being followed. There are a number of complex tasks to be implemented for SEO to be done right:

- Researching your industry, market and sales trends
- Conducting competitive research
- Finding keyword terms that can bring the most relevant traffic
- Optimizing a site
- Building links
- Monitoring and results analysis

SEO requires a well-optimized site and that can be expensive, but once completed, it continues to drive traffic without additional cost. According to Alexandra Tachalova, SEO often gets ignored when it comes to generating traffic for websites, choosing an instant boost from pay-per-click (PPC) options instead. How important is SEO to lead generation? One report says that 44% of customers begin their purchase by using a search engine and 57% of B2B marketers admit SEO has the biggest impact on lead generation. Search is the fourth top Internet activity in the US, beaten only by social media, email and video. Another report found that leads generated from search are eight times more likely to close into customers than outbound leads.

Consider also the increasing cost of AdWords because you have to keep outbidding your competitors to get top spots for visibility. Since research shows that users tend to ignore paid ad listings and click on organic results instead, focus on SEO. What's more, 80% of U.S. consumers consult online reviews before making a purchase. Even if you estimate that a small percentage would be interested in what you sell, not promoting your business online means that you're missing out on a big opportunity.

---

* Words & phrases underlined (links) are cross-referenced with URL addresses at the back

Scoop #54: Marketing strategy – more social media

Social media has been on a growth spurt and the trend is only upward. Rick Ramos says that it's only picking up speed with mobile. In his blog, "7 Statistics Every Marketer Should Know" at rickramos.com, Rick states that businesses would benefit from a marketing strategy that does more with social media.

"Businesses need to do more with content marketing if they want to make a splash and not just get wet." – **Rick Ramos**

These are the statistics cited:

- Leads generated by social media are almost double the volume than those generated by direct mail, telemarketing, trade shows, or pay-per-click campaigns, according to statistical analysis by B2B companies.
- Americans spend more than one-fourth of their Internet time on social media and social networking sites.
- More than 75% of internet users prefer to do product research on the internet prior to making a purchase.
- Web-based email traffic has been reduced by as much as 59% among young adults and teenagers, who prefer to use networks and apps like Whatsapp and instagram.
- Nine out of 10 users of email have unsubscribed from email lists and turned to networking sites.
- More than half of businesses and organizations have reported generating leads from social media.
- According to Nielsen's, almost half of internet users tend to make significant purchasing decisions based on social media.

Scoop #55: Conversion marketing

On-line marketing is all about conversion. No point spending months on engagement and then leading someone to your site, only to lose them once they're there. That's when conversion marketing kicks in by inspiring consumers who are browsing your site to make a purchase. "Conversion Marketing – Innovative Integration" at responselogic.net, explains how it plays out. When you click off of a merchant page, cancel a shopping cart, or click an external link a window pops up. It's a special offer (like free shipping or a discount). It may invite you to chat with a life agent. This is how a window shopper is converted into a paying customer.

Scoop #56: Blog posts that inform

Blogs have become very popular as a devise for attracting new followers and keeping them. People like blogs because they're informative. Blogs can substitute for or supplement a newsletter for example. There's debate over how long a blog should be. Some say about 1500 words and others say keep it to about 500 words. Whatever you do, you want to inform and not bore people. Find an angle that enlightens and doesn't just rehash what can be found readily by doing a quick search. Henneke at copyblogger.com reviews "11 Common Blogging Mistakes That Are Wasting Your Audiences Time". It's worth a read to understand these quick fixes:

1. Tell simple stories to explain complex ideas.
2. Only speak about your experiences if it helps with the message.
3. Only write when you have something to say.

* Words & phrases underlined (links) are cross-referenced with URL addresses at the back

4. Write for people and not Google crawling robots.
5. Focus on delivering your message succinctly and not word count.
6. Write so that your readers have an easy time reading your blog.
7. Write a good conclusion and not something stale.
8. Write for a reader and not a crowd.
9. Write with passion.
10. Edit. Edit. Edit.
11. Let your readers see your personality.

Scoop #57: How to promote your blog

A blog is a wonderful way to create awareness for your business but it needs promotion to work. You have to drive traffic to your blog before it can move traffic to your other sites. Rebekah Radice's blog, "8 Ideas to Boost your Latest Blog Post" at rebekahradice.com, offers some fresh ideas. Frankly, you can apply some of her ideas to you other promos:

1. Tweak your headline – It's the front door to your blog and it has to get people knocking. Your title can't be cute, clever or confusing. Edit and iterate until it's tantalizing. You can get a free analysis of the headline based on emotional, intellectual, and spiritual value, from Advanced Marketing Institute's "Emotional Marketing Value Headline Analyzer."

2. Optimize for maximum exposure – Create fresh content for your readers and Google Search. Write about current topics that are relevant to your industry. Post consistently so your readers will keep coming back. Use keywords properly. Write in a conversational language that is easy for your readers to follow. Don't write for Google.

3. Create a video – Highlight a point you made in your last blog. Keep the video short and make the sound good. No rambling.

4. Start a Google+ hangout – Hangouts On Air give you exposure in a new way and can reach a larger audience.

5. Join blog networks – Blog communities and networks help you establish relationships with fellow bloggers in your niche. Triberr, for example, can assist with building alliances. Join Tribes that share content similar to yours. Share across multiple networks immediately or set up a schedule to drip content to your social sites.

6. Use social bookmarking sites – Sharing on these sites can open your blog to millions of potential viewers. Share with some of these social bookmarking sites routinely: Reddit, Scoop.it, and StumbleUpon.

7. Turn your blog post into a podcast – Record the top tips or key takeaway for people to listen to whether they're in the car or on the treadmill. This can drive additional traffic to your sites.

8. Write a follow-up post or a series – Update blogs in your archive.

Scoop #58: Landing Page

One of the ways to drive traffic to your site is with a landing page. William Walker shares "10 Ways to Use Content Marketing to Make Your Landing Page a SureFire Hit" in his blog at digitalinformationworld.com. William states that, "It's the go-to resource for strategic marketing campaigns". What is the purpose of a landing page? If it's done properly, it can be used to:

---

* Words & phrases underlined (links) are cross-referenced with URL addresses at the back

✓ Drive people to a blog or website, where they can be persuaded to make a purchase

✓ Encourage existing customers to participate in an event, like a webinar

✓ Ask people to respond to surveys

✓ Funnel readers and group them under one single banner

✓ Promote a product or a service with a special offer

This is how to optimize your Landing Page:

1. Convince with a clear and obvious call-to-action button – subscribe, sign-up, download, purchase
2. Focus on pains and challenges – address the pains and challenges of your visitors as to compel them to click on the button
3. Be specific in your offers – too many options become confusing and drive away visitors
4. Test and evaluate how the words work – an A/B fork can tell you which slogan works best
5. Take on the targets – focus on particular stakeholders and demography with a clear message
6. Make it on time – consider the sales cycles, the season, peak hours, and client's needs
7. Impeccable use of grammar – make sure it's free of spelling and grammar errors
8. Incorporate multi-media features – images and videos relevant to copy get more engagement
9. Include the built-in incentive – must giveaway free or exclusive offers
10. Clear and concise content – use bullets and subheads to deliver content visitors can "snack on because they won't read it like a newspaper

Scoop #59: Public relations (PR) and branding

To boost your brand or reputation, you don't need to hire a public relation (PR) firm or an agency. This is how the editors of "How to Promote Your Brand" at wikihow.com (*Spaul8808, Anna, Mohini P., Lutherus*) tell you to approach PR. Understand that PR is about building relationships with the people who are using your product or services. Branding refers to a product in order to add value to the reputation. PR is about gaining exposure to a target audience with topics of interest or news. Social media networks offer a big platform for you to gain exposure.

Scoop #60: How to boost your brand

Your business stands and falls on the reputation and trust that is attributed to your brand. Both are earned over time but can be cancelled without notice. A unique brand is an asset with identity recognition. It's important that you assign your brand an inherent value and align your actions with what it represents. If you do that, your brand will blossom and your business will flourish. To boost your brand's reputation:

1. Create a message/slogan and logo that can define your business. You can toss around ideas around the kitchen table with family or friends. The slogan should encapsulate what you want the world to know. What is it that makes your business unique? What makes your business rank above competitors? Finish this statement, "Only my brand can …" Make sure your branding is the same on all your network pages. Also, identify one or two people who are best at social media and can speak to your brand. That

---

* Words & phrases underlined (links) are cross-referenced with URL addresses at the back

may not be the CEO. Someone else may be better at dealing with outside media.

2. Update your website with fresh content routinely, and make sure it loads quickly and there are no navigation issues. Visitors are not going to go to your website and remain there if the content is stale. If they have to wait to long for something to load or there's an error, they'll probably leave.

3. Connect with key media. Get in touch with reporters, broadcast, and print that cover your type of business and make sure your business is on their radar. Prepare press releases and stories they can plug in on a minute's notice. You have to spoon-feed them just like you do your followers. They are too busy and won't stop to figure out and create articles for you.

4. Attend events that showcase your industry.

Scoop #61: Benefits of social media marketing

Sometimes, if we are not seeing the desired results from our social media efforts, we start to lose heart and question whether it's all worth it. FastBrands lists the "Top 5 Benefits of Social Media Marketing" at *fast-brands.com*. These benefits emphasize the value proposition of social media that should convince you to stick to the program:

1. Social proof – given by all the likes, shares, clicks, endorsements, recommendations, follows, and so on

2. PageRank is social – the number of times a keyword is used in association with a person's name or brand determines where your blog or website is listed on the search

3. Market research – social media grows your network which provides market research for your products
4. Promotion – word of mouth marketing is more powerful than direct marketing
5. Interactive – immediate response which allows you to gage outcomes and take quick action

---

Scoop #62: Top social networking sites

The eBusiness Guide at eBiz MBA ranks the top 15 most popular social networking sites based on the average of each website's AlexaGlobal Traffic Rank, and U.S. Traffic Rank from both Compete and Quantcast. ("*#*" Denotes an estimate for sites with limited data.) This list was updated July 1, 2015:

1 | Facebook

3 - eBizMBA Rank |900,000,000- Estimated Unique Monthly Visitors |3- Compete Rank |3- Quantcast Rank |2- Alexa Rank

2 | Twitter

12 - eBizMBA Rank |310,000,000- Estimated Unique Monthly Visitors |21- Compete Rank |8- Quantcast Rank |8- Alexa Rank

3 | LinkedIn

18 - eBizMBA Rank |255,000,000- Estimated Unique Monthly Visitors |25- Compete Rank |19- Quantcast Rank |9- Alexa Rank

---

* Words & phrases underlined (links) are cross-referenced with URL addresses at the back

4 | Pinterest

22 - eBizMBA Rank |250,000,000- Estimated Unique Monthly Visitors |27- Compete Rank | 13 - Quantcast Rank |26- Alexa Rank

5 | Google Plus+

30 - eBizMBA Rank |120,000,000- Estimated Unique Monthly Visitors |*32*- Compete Rank |*28*- Quantcast Rank |NA- Alexa Rank

6 | Tumblr

34 - eBizMBA Rank |110,000,000- Estimated Unique Monthly Visitors |55- Compete Rank |*13*- Quantcast Rank |34- Alexa Rank

7 | Instagram

77 - eBizMBA Rank |100,000,000- Estimated Unique Monthly Visitors |49- Compete Rank |145- Quantcast Rank |36- Alexa Rank

8 | VK

97 - eBizMBA Rank |80,000,000- Estimated Unique Monthly Visitors |*150* - Compete Rank |*120*- Quantcast Rank |21- Alexa Rank

9 | Flickr

123 - eBizMBA Rank |65,000,000- Estimated Unique Monthly Visitors |138- Compete Rank |139- Quantcast Rank |91- Alexa Rank

10 | Vine

581 - eBizMBA Rank |42,000,000- Estimated Unique Monthly Visitors |237- Compete Rank |335- Quantcast Rank |1,172- Alexa Rank

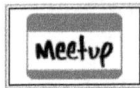

11 | Meetup

596 - eBizMBA Rank |40,000,000- Estimated Unique Monthly Visitors |791- Compete Rank |701- Quantcast Rank |296- Alexa Rank

12 | Tagged

702 - eBizMBA Rank |38,000,000- Estimated Unique Monthly Visitors |1,082- Compete Rank |615- Quantcast Rank |408- Alexa Rank

13 | Ask.fm

779 - eBizMBA Rank |37,000,000- Estimated Unique Monthly Visitors |2,046- Compete Rank |113- Quantcast Rank |179 - Alexa Rank

14 | MeetMe

1,457 - eBizMBA Rank |15,500,000- Estimated Unique Monthly Visitors |1,407- Compete Rank |635- Quantcast Rank |2,328- Alexa Rank

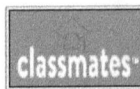

15 | ClassMates

1,487 - eBizMBA Rank |15,000,000- Estimated Unique Monthly Visitors |153- Compete Rank |*285*- Quantcast Rank |4,022- Alexa Rank

* Words & phrases underlined (links) are cross-referenced with URL addresses at the back

Scoop #63: 61 Best social media tools for small business

I started out saying that information is power. But information overload can swamp you, unless you take control. This is why I'm going to lead you to a blog where you can find tools that will make your life simpler. Really! I wish someone told me about some of these tools when I started. Kevin Lee's blog, "The Big List of The 61 Best Social Media Tools for Small Business " at blog.bufferapp.com, itemizes and categorizes the best 61 social media tools for small business. You will find tools that help you create content, ones that help you sort out followers, and ones that help you monitor social media buzz. There are dashboards and plug-ins, translation and design services, and so much more. You have to check it out.

Scoop #64: Make sure Google can find your site

Denis Label's post on "Create a Great Site & Have it Found in Google" at +Denis Label has some useful links for search results:

- Google Webmaster: google.com/webmasters/
- Support/Help: support.google.com/webmasters
- On YouTube: youtube.com/GoogleWebmasterhelp
- On Google+: +Google Webmasters

Scoop #65: Top tips from successful people

Sometimes we just need some inspiration. An infographic on "Everyday Billionaires" at *growtheverywhere.com* captures the top tips from successful people for building a solid lifestyle. People want to know how successful people made it to the top and learn what they can to boost their own success. You've undoubtedly heard that it's not what you know but who you know that gets you ahead. Getting tips from top billionaires is an insider's scoop.

1. Warren Buffet advises us to make a rule to stay on the side of the minority. He says, "Get worried when people start to agree with you. Read a lot." He also advises us to not rush it or get greedy.

2. Larry Ellison advises to ignore the critics.

3. David Koch states that markets are driven by psychology and not reality. He tells us to learn how to diversify.

4. George Soros says he's only rich because he knows when he's wrong and also warns that friendship based on business is better than business based on friendship.

5. Bill Gates advises us to bite off more than we can chew. He lets us in on a secret, "Life is not fair, get used to it."

6. Richard Branson says, "Having savvy is far more important than formal education." He reminds us, "Don't promise what you can't deliver and deliver everything you promise."

7. Mark Zuckerberg says, "Don't let anyone tell the story of you," and "You are only as strong as the team around you."

8. Carlos Slim advises, "Think both positively and possibly," and "Understand the Future and Your Place in it."

---

* Words & phrases underlined (links) are cross-referenced with URL addresses at the back

Scoop #66: Persistence pays off

Persistence is the key to success. When success doesn't come fast enough or when it costs too much, we want to give up. It usually comes down to expectations. If you expect your goal to be realized within six months and it doesn't happen, you get impatient. Ask yourself are your expectations too high? In "The Most Motivating Video for Success" on *YouTube*, Steve Jobs said, "You have to have passion for what you're doing...because it's so hard... And you have to do it over a sustained period of time." It may be easier to give up but living with a bruised ego is not fun. Failure is not easily forgotten. Not realizing our dreams leads to regret. So give it a good go before quitting and don't stop believing. Ultimately if you are determined you will succeed in life.

More on Content Marketing

Scoop #67: What are most businesses doing?

Sure it's easy to talk about content marketing in general but what's everyone actually doing? Simply put – not enough. Businesses would do well to heed the advice of Rick Ramos because it's borne out by the facts. +BoostSuite asked 16,000+ small business owners and content marketers about their content marketing strategies. They summed up the results in an infographic, "The State of Small Business Content Marketing in 2014" at smallbusiness.yahoo.com. While businesses are doing basic content marketing, the process is disjointed and ineffective. Mostly they're blogging, networking on social media, and doing email marketing; all based on their gut feeling. They conclude that small business can achieve exceptional results by using data-driven marketing tools that will connect them with partners. This will help businesses grow their audience and generate more leads. This is the small-business strategy being used:

1. Content marketing is web-based – 89% publishing weekly, mostly blogging.
2. Content marketing is time-consuming – 5% of the work week is used to create web content (over half spend 2 hours per piece of content).

* Words & phrases underlined (links) are cross-referenced with URL addresses at the back

3. Content marketing is random – 86% don't use data to make smart decisions.
4. Email marketing is under-utilized – 65% send a newsletter.
5. Content differs based on the channel – 81% create different content for web vs. social vs. email and are missing out on being consistent.
6. Small businesses are not working with anyone else – 74% have never worked with a partner; missing out on building back-links.
7. Solo-marketing doesn't work anymore – do-it-together approach generates larger and more engaged audiences, back-links, and builds authority.
8. There's a huge opportunity to use data to get better marketing results – working smarter is better than working harder.

Scoop #68: Content strategy – checklist

A recipe for serving up great content is found on econsultancy.com. James Carson's blog, "The 24 ingredients for a delicious content strategy" is recommended reading. He divides the 24 ingredients into four bowls: analytics, site structure, content and distribution, and gives you specifics on what to do and how to do it.

1. Website engagement analytics – what content drives the most traffic
2. Website organic traffic information – which keywords and content are driving traffic to your site
3. Keyword analysis – what tools to use to find high-rank keywords and brainstorm
4. Content mind map – how to outline categories and articles for your content

5. SEO and social competitor map analysis - how to spot-check competitors' sites for content search-ability

6. Category card sort – how to review the stack of content already written

7. Tagging amendments – how to improve the tags (keywords) your pages to match search "profiles" which are not redundant

8. Menu restructure – how to build menus which help users find your content

9. SEO on page – how to check if your content is good for SEO

10. Evergreen content audit – how to keep content fresh

11. Retrospective editing – what to do with older content

12. Authorship review – how to get the author's face on SEO markup for Google search

13. Taxonomy and audit phase goals – how to optimize content for your site

14. Stock and flow – how to use feed stream and original content to remain relevant

15. Page types – what type of pages will be produced regularly: blog, product review, etc.

16. Editorial calendar – how to schedule production

17. Quantitative benchmarking system – how to score your content along metrics (signals) relevant to your business

18. Headlines – how to write headlines for the web

19. Formatting – how to format content for the web

20. Distributable content – what content is best for the web

21. Social media – how to do more than just post and expand your strategy for social media

22. Email – how to make the most of email marketing

23. Partner network – how to create "win-win" associations on the web

* Words & phrases underlined (links) are cross-referenced with URL addresses at the back

24. Paid for network – how to push your content with paid exposure

---

Scoop #69: How to promote content – the big picture

What is the best way to promote content on the web? That's the million dollar question that everyone wants answered. Creating content is the easy part. Distributing it is the hard part! Promoting it effectively requires a holistic approach which has to be part of your overall marketing strategy. Trying different tricks or throwing a bunch of content against the wall to see what sticks is not sensible and only leads to frustration. Consider that you can access many communities and platforms – Facebook Twitter, LinkedIn, Reddit, YouTube, and industry forums. Ask yourself who would want to read this content and where can I find those people? Knowing how best to syndicate your content can result in many more eyeballs and potential conversions.

But first you have to figure out your marketing and sales goals as they relate to SEO objectives, potential sales results you might generate with PPC and banner advertising or paid placement in emails, newsletters, etc. Are you after email sign ups, user sign ups, or lead generation?

Social media is one way to go but you should consider email outreach, backlink building, and syndication. You would also want to leverage your existing network of vendors, suppliers, business partners, and collaborators to generate the best content and help amplify your message. Also, there may be some opportunities sitting in your customer data files that can be excavated. When you're coming up with an approach consider the following:

1. Who is your target audience and where do they hang out? The answer will direct you to advertise or reach out via social media, bloggers, or industry journalists, for example.

2. What content can you generate that is really, really good? Make sure your content is "contagious" and "share-worthy". Not sales dribble or corporate speak but useful to clients, competitors and influencers. Use that content to build links and raise awareness about your product or expertise. If it's really awesome, they'll link to it and share it. You can also get your network to link and share it with their networks. If you present it to a big enough crowd, it will get shared. Here are some ideas on how you can generate awesome content:
   - Find an article that already performed well in your niche (search on BuzzSumo)
   - Figure out what makes it so good and generate better content on the same theme
   - Find everyone who linked to the original article or shared it. Reach out and share your content with them

3. Once you hit on content that resonates and engages your target audience, expand on it. Create an infographic, a video or slide presentation. Develop an e-book from a blog. Squeeze as much value out of that awesome content as you can.

4. Perform a content analysis of existing assets to discover what content is the most influential in generating leads – an attribution report analysis. The report will help you decide the next steps. Look at your most valuable content assets and sort them according to smaller themes. Are there any trends or insights that you can use?
   - Is 20% of your content generating 80% of your site's total traffic or sales?

* Words & phrases underlined (links) are cross-referenced with URL addresses at the back

- What are the traffic sources for the different themes or content?
- How engaging are your site visitors with different types of content on your website?
- Are the search queries used by visitors arriving from search engines matching the website content where they landed?
- When was your top performing content created? Is it time to update it?
- Is search or social media driving more traffic and conversion on your website?

5. Reach out to influencers in your niche that will find your content relevant and useful enough for their audience. Great content will make them look good and that's a great incentive for them to share.

6. Guest blogging is a good backup plan if influencers in your industry rarely link to other websites. Find those blogs that have a highly engaged audience and create valuable and useful content tailored to their audience. Your post ideas should be an extension of the content that you already have on your website. Start with an infographic, for example. Track the quantity and quality of traffic coming from guest blogging so you can decide to continue or not.

7. Repurpose your content into new packets with different consumption formats. It's a proven way of bringing in traffic because you are essentially spreading your content in front of more eyeballs.

8. Update old blog content so it's fresh and up-to-date and it can generate more traffic and conversion. Hubspot calls this historical optimization and reports that they more than doubled the monthly leads off optimized posts and increased monthly organic search views of old posts on average by 106%.

9. Great content assets with clear calls to action buttons for viewing and downloading can drive leads and conversion.

10. Blogging can help increase visibility of your content by as much as 20% month over month if you're blogging daily. To do that you would need content management automation.

11. This is what you can do:
   - Rub shoulders with the experts
   - Send newsletters
   - Say hello to press releases
   - Go guest post
   - Share on social media websites
   - Targeted sharing: mention people who already follow you
   - Bookmark it on social bookmarking sites
   - Q&A sites: LinkedIn Answers, quora.com, focus.com
   - Post a summary on niche social sites
   - Email marketing
   - Align the post with a key phrase
   - Link to the post from other posts

Get more expert advice on this topic in Scoop 81 – Content that sells.

Scoop #70: Engagement gap – Facebook vs. Google Plus vs. Twitter

Charts and figures results for "Q1 2014 U.S. Top Brands Social WebTrack" by *Forrester* looked at over 2,500 posts on social platforms by top brands. It shows that the gap in engagement is quite narrow between Facebook and Google+, with Twitter a distant third. Forrester found that 22% of U.S. online adults say they use Google+ at least once a month, the same as Twitter. A comparison of interaction on brand posts showed that Google+ users on average interacted almost as much as Facebook users (0.069% vs. 073%) and twice as much as Twitter users (0.035%), i.e., likes (+1s) and comments.

Kevin Lee at blog.bufferapp.com mentions that Buffer's social-media audits of their fans indicate that they get twice the engagement on Google+ than on Facebook.

Scoop #71: The case for Google Plus

The report, "The Case for Google Plus" by *Forrester,* notes that there are benefits to the Google Plus platform, derived from SEO. Google features Google+ brand posts on the right-hand side of its search-results page and Google+ posts may help boost PageRank for users who follow the brand on the social network. Zap Stambor's blog, "Is Google Plus More Important than Twitter?" at *internetretailer.com,* says that despite those benefits, 12 of the 50 large brands Forrester examines in its "Q1 2014 U.S. Top Brands Social WebTrack" report don't have an official Google Plus Page. Another six built Pages but did not post to them in February, when the survey was done. Nate Elliott, Vice President, Principal Analyst at Forrester says that these are missed opportunities.

> *"I believe every marketer should use Google Plus."*
> — **Nate Elliott, Forrester**

Two ways that brands can boost engagement:

1. Post the same content on both Facebook and Google+. That helped retailers like Louis Vuitton generate above average engagement (0.112% Google Plus vs. 0.099% Facebook)

2. Promote Google+ accounts on other websites, in e-mails everywhere they promote their Facebook, Twitter and Pinterest accounts

Zap Stambor says that many large online retailers are not doing these two things, according to data available on Internet Retailer's Top500Guide.com. For example, network share buttons makes it easy for shoppers to share products with their friends on social networks. But most don't even show a share button on their sites. A comparison of how many of the largest online merchants in North America display the share button on their product Pages, reveals that Google Plus buttons are lagging:

- 266 out of 500 feature the Google+ "+1" button
- 308 out of 500 feature a Pinterest "Pin It" button
- 326 out of 500 feature the Twitter "Tweet" button
- 496 out of 500 feature the Facebook's "Like" button

Scoop #72: Business benefits of using Google Plus

Lynnette Young of Purple Stripe is a marketing expert with more than 1.5 million followers on Google+. She was interviewed by Michael Stelzner of SocialMedia Marketing about how businesses can use the tools on Google+ to succeed.

1. Google has about 60 products and Google+ is the one that links all of them together.

> *"When you are in the Google ecosystem, it's where you live for search, email, videos, etc."*
> – **Lynnette Young, Purple Stripe**

2. What marketers need to know about Google+ users – Google+ is more like Twitter or Reddit, not in how you publish but how the communities separate themselves

---

* Words & phrases underlined (links) are cross-referenced with URL addresses at the back

and group together. It's easier to reach these communities on Google+ than it is on Facebook. Google+ has a community for every niche.

"As a marketer this is what you want. If you want to get your message out, you obviously want to gravitate toward people you know will meet your criteria and will hopefully want your product." – **Lynnette Young, Purple Stripe**

3. Published content takes a different path on Google+ than on Facebook – the longer content exists on Google+ and the longer people continue to interact with it, the more it will show up near the top of the Google Search page.

4. How to get your content to show up in search on Google+ – make sure that when you post great content, people can find it quickly. Construct your content in a way that Google understands or it will pass you by:

   ▪ Learn how *Google authorship* and *Google Publisher* work and how your data needs to be structured.
   ▪ Research how to use *Google Analytics* to track everything you do.
   ▪ Get more traction on Google+ by learning about and using as many Google products as you need.
   ▪ Make sure your website is solid. Have a working understand of Schema.org

5. Can you post the exact same updates on Facebook and Google+ and expect similar results? You can build and grow a more sustainable level of engagement on Google+ compared to Facebook.

   ▪ Lynette explains that once people like your page on Facebook, you have to fight to keep their attention. You have to post high-impact, sensationalized content to grab them each time.

- Storyline-driven content is harder on Facebook because your followers might not see the entire story. If they skip one piece, you miss the chance to lead them to the call to action at the end of the tunnel. Whereas in Google+, you can build a narrative because each piece of content will stay there forever until you take it down.
- Create content on Google+ which has more of everything – video, large images, and GIFs.
- You can tell a story differently on Google+ so use media types different from those you would use on other platforms.

6. Other tips for content on Google+ – with solid content and a solid message look at different and unique ways to publish your content.
    - Use interactive posts (loosely compared to a Twitter card).
    - Use Hangouts and live streams. Lynnette says she's even seen Twitter chats scheduled inside Google+ events.
    - Brick-and-mortar businesses can make use of Google Maps.
    - Use hashtags – Google+ even adds them for you. It's a huge search tool.
    - On Google+ you can edit a post after it's been published but not on Twitter. You can't change the visibility level on Facebook. This can help you "resurrect your one-time evergreen content and reactivate it."

7. A company that's doing it right on Google+ – RedEnvelope promoted a live red carpet event on Google+ with great use of multimedia that wouldn't be possible elsewhere.

RedEnvelope posted content on it, did videos and also held live Q&A with the audience.

Scoop #73: Google Plus marketing tips

Cindy King's blog "5 Google+ Marketing Tips from the Pros" features tips from top Google+ experts:

1. "Close off Google+ Comments to Increase Engagement", by Martin Shervington. Martin suggests disabling comments on your Google+ posts as a way of "punctuating people's attention". Since everyone who comments gets notifications of follow-up comments, this trick gives you "the last word". Use this method to announce the next step in your campaign, for example. Next, add those people who have engaged with you to your circles and build relationships with them. You can enable the comments when you have something new to announce and want to market to people who related to your post previously.

2. Leverage people's hovercards to grow your audience, by Ryan Hanley. Ryan points out that people leave a trail of what they like, say, and do with their signature 'hovercards'. Every click (+1 or share) and comment that people make on Google+ gets recorded. He suggests that you don't have to rely solely on generating new content if you use 'hovercards' to find people you want to engage for your business or brand. Search for these people using the Google+ Search bar and then engage with them and add them to your circles.

3. Schedule your Google+ posts for maximum impact, by Ian Cleary. Ian suggests publishing your valuable content over

time rather than all at once. He recommends using the free Chrome DoShare plugin to share content at a time that suits your audience. This plugin allows you to easily add the content you wish to share to a queue.

4. Use your Google+ Profile to claim authorship of your content, by Kristi Hines. Kristi suggests that you claim authorship of every blog and publication you write, regardless of whether you have a website or not. She also recommends signing up for Google Webmaster Tools using the same google account as your Google+ Profile. This will allow you to see analytics data for the posts linked to your Google+ Profile, under the Labs menu for Author Stats. Since you can't get analytics for your content other than on your own sites, you will get insight on the popularity of your content.

5. Make sure your images take up significant real estate, by Marcela De Vivo. Marcela suggests that you go the extra step and share images that are "tall and skinny" with people and attractive colors. Her #1 tip is to not allow Google+ to grab an image from the link in your post. Experiment with different sizes and colors to see what works best and if you find images that are not the right size, use a tool like Canva or PicMonkey to resize and make them look appealing. Her final tip is to offer charts and graphs in your posts and make statistics part of your content. Since this is not done often, it will make you a leader and lead to more likes and shares.

---

* Words & phrases underlined (links) are cross-referenced with URL addresses at the back

Scoop #74: Search tips for Google Plus posts

Google is a powerful search engine but finding what you need on the Google Plus platform is not always easy. Some posts have a long trail, and specifics about each post and related activity gets buried. For example, you may want to dig up a particular conversation on a post or look up the last time you published that post so you don't spam. Also, you may want to monitor activity on posts by your competitors or people of influence. Stephan Hovnanian wrote a blog, "Search tips within Google Plus" at websighthangouts.com. His tips on how to use the "Peoples and Pages" search bar at the top of the Google+ window can save you a lot of time.

Scoop #75: Google Hangouts On Air – Getting viewers

Another valuable resource found at socialmediaexaminer.com is Ryan Hanley's blog, "10 Ways to Get Live Viewers for Your Google Hangouts on Air". Here is the checklist of what you can do to promote your Hangouts On Air:

1. Use consistent branding
2. Create eye-catching headlines
3. Keep track of your audience
4. Go for friends of friends
5. Add audience reminders
6. Make the most of your teaser video
7. Collect the conversation with hashtags
8. Make it easy with mobile users
9. Give your audience options
10. Hang out in the comments

Scoop #76: Content marketing – mistakes

It's helpful to look at basic mistakes that we may be making in our content marketing strategy. We can learn equally as much from what people do wrong as what they do right. Robert M. Brecht's blog, "Are You Making these 7 Direct Marketing Mistakes?" at dmn3.com is a good place to start. I can see how the same mistakes made in direct marketing can be made in content marketing. These are 7 *content* marketing mistakes and their implications:

1. Buying a list of followers or sharing mega-circles which are not curated can lead to lots of frustration.
2. Targeting too broadly leads to wasted energy and budget dollars. Use data-driven marketing tools to segment your audience and target more narrowly your campaigns.
3. Not integrating across multiple channels – your message should be consistent and integrated across all channels – direct mail and off-line tactics along with web and social media channels
4. Not creating enough touches – a minimum of three touches is necessary and five to seven is considered ideal.
5. Not using both emotional and rational appeal – consumers buy with emotion and justify with rational information.
6. Focusing on the product instead of the prospect – answer the customer's question, "what's in it for me?" and don't use appeals that are vendor-oriented.
7. Not doing continuous testing and refinement – campaigns improve with ongoing testing and evaluation and an ongoing and controlled testing program will achieve better results.

Scoop #77: The customer-business relationship

The sad state of affairs, is that with all the tools available for customer engagement and everything we know about content marketing, customers are more easily disappointed than ever, according to a report, "Engagement 3.0: A New Model for Customer Engagement" at *thunderhead.com*.

They advise that it's important to refine the customer-business relationship. Jim Tierney quotes the report in his blog, "Redefining Customer Engagement in the Digital Era" at loyalty360.org, as stating that over half the customers didn't see any improvement in the customer-business relationship over the prior three years.

Moreover, customers will judge a business more critically now and are less willing to forgive. If something goes wrong, they will act more decisively. According to the report, businesses face three major challenges:

1. Communication which doesn't relate to customers' needs
2. Cannot keep pace with customer expectation
3. Disjointed communication caused by company silos

What steps can a business take to improve the customer-business relationship?

- Remove organizational barriers to the customer experience
- Learn from every interaction and refine the process
- Get everyone in the business on the same page, ready to treat the customer personal with real time customer records.

How to Craft Content

Scoop #78: Content stream

Recent studies reveal that what marketers want to learn most is how to craft original visual content for their inbound marketing campaigns. Content is the main fuel used to drive the marketing machine. You score a home run when a content piece runs viral and that's what everyone wishes for. But you can win the game with persistence too and marketers know that. To do it requires content assets that score an A+ consistently. Since there are a lot of talented people working very hard to gain followers and create awareness about their business, you have to up your game to compete for eyeballs in social media and the internet. How do you do that?

The scoops that follow expand on what you've already learned about content marketing in previous sections and fill in some gaps. To get an overview of type of content to consider review the stats below, which show trends. Then go about producing content that gets an A+ on the quality scale. That means it's findable, readable, actionable, and shareable. Broadly speaking, focus on delivering content that is informative, inspiring, and interactive, and your message will be heard above the noise. For example, invite people to give their opinions, share ideas, and help somehow. Involve them in your research or surveys. Invite them

* Words & phrases underlined (links) are cross-referenced with URL addresses at the back

to participate in upcoming events and competitions. Tell them something they don't already know. Add or reshape content and give it a new spin.

To get clicks your content has to get ranked highly so that it shows up in a social stream and in search results. The more people click on it, the higher the ranking. It's a circular loop that expands more and more with engagement. It's like throwing a stone in the water and then watching the ripples form. But to get the most ripples your content has to be shaped just right. You have to produce content assets that get people excited about the story you deliver. Keep in mind that we are hard wired for rewards so give people an incentive for doing what you ask. It's not what you say but how you say it. It's not how great your product is but how you make your followers feel about it. Your content should be sticky (fun and easy). It should be trustworthy. It should be current.

As discussed in previous sections, every major social network including Facebook, Twitter, LinkedIn, and Instagram is giving visual content more importance in terms of their ranking algorithm. That's because research data shows that adding videos, photos, and links all result in an impressive boost to engagement.

Douglas Mason at Twitter Blog analyzed millions of Tweets for 2014 sent by verified users in the United States in the areas of government, music, news, sports and TV, in order to evaluate the difference made by photos, hashtags, links, videos, and tweets containing a number or digit (i.e. sports scores or an official stat). They wanted to know why certain tweets saw higher average engagement and were able to confirm that adding visual content boosted retweets as follows:

- Photos – 35% average boost
- Videos – 28% boost

- Quotes – 19% boost
- Including a number – 17% boost
- Hashtags – 16% boost

Twitter Blog also found that results vary by industry. For example, in TV it's one result and in Sports it's something else. The charts show the results of a selection of tweet features, which vary by industry. You can review the industry results more closely by navigating to the URL addresses given at the back of the book for these links: <u>TV</u>|<u>News</u>|<u>Music</u>|<u>Government & Politics</u>|<u>Sports</u>

There is no question that visual content boosts engagement and that's why the trend is towards using more of it. Marketers design their content marketing assets with visual content and you should consider doing the same. Jesse Mawhinney's blog at hubspot.com discusses "17 Stats You Should Know About Visual Content Marketing in 2015". Jesse makes the point that visual content is used significantly by marketers to increase "blog traffic, social media engagement, visitor-to-lead conversion rates and inbound customer acquisition results".

Jesse reviewed several studies conducted in 2014 and says that research data confirms the "amazing effectiveness of visual content for social media". He cites stats that make this point 17 times for B2B and B2C marketing:

1. Video posts per person on Facebook grew 75% (3.6X) year over year and video content.
2. Tweets with images received 18% more clicks, 89% more favorites, and 150% more retweets.
3. Posts with photos on Facebook brand pages had more engagement and accounted for 87% of total interactions. (A review of the top 10% of posts made by more than 30,000 Socialbakers.com)

* Words & phrases underlined (links) are cross-referenced with URL addresses at the back

4. 39% of B2B buyers indicated they shared infographics frequently on social media.
5. Adding a photo URL to your tweet, you can boost retweets by 35% (as indicated above).
6. Images and photos are most important for optimizing social media posts.
7. Visual content is a key component in the top 5 B2B marketing tactics.
8. 70% of marketers planned to increase their use of original visual assets.
9. B2B buyers look for whitepapers (78%), case studies (73) and webinars (67%) when making a purchase decision.
10. B2C marketers are more likely to use original videos and original visual content (63% B2C vs. 56% B2B for each type)
11. B2B buyers prefer shorter content formats (95%).
12. 86% of buyers wanted interactive/visual content on demand.
13. Social Media Examiner found that what marketers wanted most was to learn how to create original visual content.
14. In 2014, video content for B2B marketing increased by 8% to 58% while infographics increased by 9% to 52%.
15. Interactive content formats (Brainshark, SlideShare) increased in popularity from 21% in 2013 to 28% in 2014.
16. B2B marketers are using 12 to 14 formats of content on average.
17. B2B marketers are shifting are shifting preference from whitepapers to video.

Scoop #79: First impression – color

First impressions are key to the perception that a visitor forms about your brand and color plays a big role in that. How do you choose the colors for your profile, website, and blog that will show off your brand and make the most impact? "Design Essential Series" at dustn.tv is a guide for choosing brand colors for your blog. Your brand colors should be the same for all your sites. The trend with major brands is to use two or three colors, so follow their lead. If you are unsure about how to combine colors there are tools to help you or you can hire a graphics designer:

- Decide on two primary colors and one accent color
- Find a perfect color palette on colourlovers.com or Kuler.Adobe.com
- Stick to these colors on all your sites and the brand will stick in people's minds

Scoop #80: Content on a shoe string

Can you get quality content on a shoe-string budget? Yes you can. While it may be frustrating to not have the budget to buy quality content, it is possible to do more with less. It is worth considering that content marketing costs 62% less than traditional marketing and generates three times the leads. Henry Adose' blog, "10 Tips for creating Content on a Limited Budget" at www.dmn3.com, gives 10 low-cost ideas you can use to create new content:

1. Repurpose – transform existing content into new content
2. Solicit guest posts
3. Ask – get input from readers
4. Beg – get team members to contribute
5. Interview customers

* Words & phrases underlined (links) are cross-referenced with URL addresses at the back

6. Profile – a team member with a great story
7. Share a case study
8. Publish a research report
9. Analyze a report
10. Curate interesting stories

Scoop #81: Content that sells

How do you create content that sells your products or services? I'll answer this question in three parts.

PART 1) Get down to basics – develop a template.
Erick's blog at responselogic.net is an "E-Commerce Product Page Writing Tutorial" that outlines how to go about it. Start with smart keywords:

1. Sign out of your Google account and do a Google search for your product. Look at the bottom of the search results page for the section on "related searches". Here you find possible keywords to use in your copy. You can also use the *Keyword Planner* in Google AdWords. Also research your competition for ideas.
2. Next, come up with the title tag using the best keywords only. Don't overdo it.
3. Come up with something unique for your product description. Focus on benefits or solutions and not on features. Use these questions to help you:
   a. Who is using the product?
   b. What are the circumstances they are using it for?
   c. Why do they need it?
   d. Where is it going?
   e. When should they have this product?

Do's and Don'ts:

- Don't omit the manufacturer's specs or facts!
- Don't mention shipping or handling in the text as it may hurt your pay-per-click ads!
- ✓ Do provide a lengthy description for a product over $100 – longer than the manufacturer's specs.
- ✓ Do Add an ALT tag or keyword description to every photo – it helps with accessibility and Google Search.

PART 2) Become a ghostwriter – write for the target audience.

The key to writing content that sells is to approach it from the customer's perspective. When Terry Palmer interviewed Felicia Sphar, Direct-Response Copywriter and Founder of Instantly Irresistible, she told him a secret:

"Hardly anyone will tell you this, but writing great copy is all about stealing. Literally, stealing the words from your customers' mouths... which is why asking survey questions is so important. One of my favorites to ask that performs consistently well is: "If you had this information, what would it allow you to do? How would you feel?" I love to ask this question via email because people really open up, have time to think through their answers, and you'll find a lot of 'gold nuggets' for your copy.

"This is how you get the 'painted picture' of what your product actually means to someone—as it's never about the product itself. You have to uncover what's 'under the rug' in order to move people with any copy you write—and then USE that exact language. Thankfully, there are no 'copy police' that get you for stealing. You're only rewarded in sales." **– Felicia Sphar**

PART 3) Make them an offer they can't refuse.

Persuading people to "buy" requires a strategy. It may take a lot of doing to get someone to pay attention but once they do, you can help them make a quick decision. Develop your content using proven behavioral psychology. Tim Ash explains the use of

* Words & phrases underlined (links) are cross-referenced with URL addresses at the back

neuromarketing principles as the "simple application of behavioral psychology to create low stress, low friction websites that provide a pleasant user experience and result in higher engagement". According to Tim:

> *"Neuromarketing works because of the simple fact that the human brain relies on shortcuts to efficiently process the thousands of decisions it is forced to make on a given day. Scientists have been able to identify many of these shortcuts, which is a boon to marketers looking to persuade consumers to make a purchase decision."* – **Tim Ash**

My version of this is that if you make it easy and fun, it's a win-win. Tim discusses six proven techniques that you can use to get your target audience to respond favorably to your sales tactics:

1. Leverage scarcity to persuade a visitor to buy now – we want what we can't have. Something in short supply (limited quantity) or a time-limited offer or an expiry on price discount is a tactic that can influence the buying decision. Also, we don't want to risk losing out. If the buyer feels they can postpone making the decision, they will. "People have a natural aversion to loss – they'd rather act too hastily... than risk missing out."

2. Use a decoy to steer visitors toward a certain product – give users options A or B. Because the human brain is wired to compare things, we don't know what we want unless we see it in context. When you present a decoy – a less desirable choice – for comparison, the product you want to sell looks better. For example, if item A is $500 and B is $1,000, add C at $1,500 to get people to consider B as reasonable or "less expensive".

3. Use anchoring to help visitors justify their selection – the first piece of information presented is the anchor or the marker for comparison. Use this bias to help visitors justify

their purchase selection. For example, the initial price given for a used car becomes the anchor for negotiations, so that lower prices seem more reasonable even if the initial price was high.

4. Make visitors feel indebted to you – people are driven to repay debts no matter how small. It's the rule of reciprocity. Use this impulse to spur visitors to act. By giving something of value with no expectation, you can harness their goodwill. Offer exclusive information, free samples, or a free home trial. Offer free advice, a buyer's guide. Test giving visitors a portion of a whitepaper rather than asking them to fill out a form. Make a genuine gesture without any manipulation.

5. Offer items you don't expect to sell to help you sell lower priced options – start with an unreasonable option, e.g. VIP tickets at $1,300. When the visitor signals they are not interested and are about to leave the page or hit the "No thanks" button, present another offer at a lower price, e.g. regular ticket at $500. Apparently, this is better than if you just presented the $500 item. The second items looks more reasonably priced in contrast to the first option. Tim says this principle works well for fundraising and volunteer services.

6. Use the hurt and rescue principle – show them they have a problem and then offer to fix it. The diet industry uses this principle all the time by pointing out all the health risks and then offering plans (food and exercise options) as cures. This technique also works for B2B marketing. Point out how much money or time a business is wasting and offer a solution.

Scoop #82: Swimming with the pros

Arnie Kuen at marketingland.com, wrote a magnificent blog, "Top Tips for Optimizing Your Content: 9 Experts Weigh In". As more advertisers turn to online marketing, the content stream grows, and it gets harder to find your content. There is also a struggle between content optimized for Google Search and content that caters to your followers. The best tips from thse 9 experts are given in the scoops below.

Scoop #83: Content optimization – QUART test

The best tip for content optimization from Alan Bleiweiss (alanbleiweiss.com) is to use the QUART test to score content: Quality, Uniqueness, Authority, Relevance, Trust. Alan says the #1 mistake people make is to get fixated on signals like inbound links, keyword usage, crawl efficiency, content depth, etc. Alan advises focusing on quality, uniqueness, and authority. He says that becoming myopic, leads to content which feels artificially fed and opens the door to competitors. Focus on quality, uniqueness, and authority to spread your energy, effort, and resources around.

Scoop #84: Content optimization – keywords

Keyword optimization is extremely important for generating free organic traffic to your blog or website. Keywords are special words or phrases used by search engines for relevant web pages. When a user requests a search, the search engine (e.g. Google, Bing, and Yahoo) has to index relevant pages before listing them in search results. The search algorithm looks at keywords and content relevance as well as backlinks and other SEO factors, to index the document. It's no wonder that top marketers mention keyword optimization as their #1 content optimization tip.

David Wallace (searchrank.com) advises researching keywords or phrases to sprinkle in your content. He confirms it can help with ranking and driving traffic to your site. Also, he says, optimize the title tag and if you're going to add a brand to it, attach it at the end of the tag. He adds that you should use the title and ALT attributes for the images and if there is an infographic, include an "Embed Code" snippet below the graphic.

Eric Enge (marketingland.com) advises doing the research to figure out what keywords users use most often when discussing the topic of your content. He suggests using the keywords to help you decide on the focus of your content and the title of the article. Then let writers write naturally and don't cramp them with targets for stuffing the copy with keyword variants. "Creating content that meets the user's needs should be your number one goal," says Eric. Don't over think it! Let writers write and they will produce semantically rich content that people want to read.

Uprise.io is a content marketing tool that allows you to research and analyze top performing content in different industries. They gathered data on nearly 500,000 articles published from January 1 to April 30, 2015. Using this tool, Hubspot researched the most common keywords found in the top shared articles on Facebook, Twitter, LinkedIn, Google+, and Pinterest for about a dozen categories.

For example, the most common keywords for the analytics category include: how to, google analytics, infographic, marketing, simplify, brand, data, reporting, and Pinterest.

---

* Words & phrases underlined (links) are cross-referenced with URL addresses at the back

Another example - the most common keywords for the content marketing category include: content, marketing, infographic, how to, ways, media, tips, google, business, key, and online.

Scoop #85: Content optimization – goals

The best tip on content optimization from Melissa Fach (twitter.com/seaware) is to have SEO and business goals and strategies, "Goals give direction and effective strategies give results." Content should be created to meet the goals of the site. The strategy for each piece of content should be to develop trust, meet needs, and create urgency. Without trust you have nothing. If you don't meet a need - you are not needed, and urgency doesn't allow customers to slip away. Melissa points out that getting more traffic accomplishes nothing without conversion, "It is critical that the content be focused on converting a website visitor into a customer."

Scoop #86: Content optimization – surveys

The best tip on content optimization from Rand Fishkin (moz.com) is to survey a sample of your followers that may be interested in the topic of your content. Get their input. Find out what they're curious about and what specifically they'd like you to address. Is there an information gap? If you write about something they're interested in, you've struck gold. If your content doesn't fill that gap, you need to rethink it. Rand says that the #1 mistake people make is to assume that just because you built it, people will come. He emphasizes that getting the content "right" takes a lot of effort and years of practice, and even failed attempts.

Chloe Mason Gray specializes in digital marketing and growth strategy for small businesses and solopreneurs. Chloe states that "all great marketing starts with a deep understanding of your customer" and reminds us of the importance of consistent market research. There are lots of great tools to help you create a survey but there is an art to gathering "actionable data that gives you deep insights" into your target market. And with practice you'll get good at it and have enough traffic and subscriber data so you can automate the process for a constant flow of current data. Chloe's blog at kissmetrics.com, "7 Experts Tell You How To Create Winning Marketing Surveys" is an excellent resource that will help you develop your marketing surveys. Chloe interviewed these experts and they elaborate on the pointers listed here:

1. Peep Laja, Founder of Markitekt and ConversionXL — The best online surveys are qualitative
2. Felicia Sphar, Direct-Response Copywriter and Founder of Instantly Irresistible — Use surveys to steal words from your customers' mouths
3. Chuck Liu, User Experience Research Manager at KISSmetrics — Use surveys to benchmark visitors' primary motivation for being on your site
4. Meghan Lockwood, Senior Manager of Content Strategy at edynamic — Before you send out your survey, make sure to have outside eyes read it
5. Kristi Hines, Freelance Writer, Social Media Expert & Blogger — Build a big list of topic ideas for your content marketing with on-page surveys
6. Rebecca Corliss, Inbound Marketing Manager at HubSpot — — Use surveys to run successful inbound marketing campaigns

---

* Words & phrases underlined (links) are cross-referenced with URL addresses at the back

7. Sherice Jacob, Writer and Founder of iElectirfy— Difficult questions can lead your prospect to abandon your survey

---

Scoop #87: Content optimization – readability

The best tip from AJ Kohn (searchengineland.com) is simple: readability. "Don't make your users work for your content. People don't generally read. They scan." Use strong font, interesting subheads, short paragraphs, and images to break up the content. "Make people remember," is how he puts it. The #1 mistake people make according to AJ is to give up too soon.

Scoop #88: Content optimization – page title

The best tip from Dr. Pete Meyers (moz.com) is to put more time and effort into page titles. Limit the title to 55 characters and don't stuff it with keywords. Start with words optimized for Google Search and for impact. Create short titles that will lead to relevant clicks. Dr. Pete notes that "If you have to repeat title elements across your site (like a category or site name), put the unique elements first. The #1 mistake, he says, is that people want every page on their site to be indexed and that leads to dilution and ranking confusion. He has the same issue with internal links. "Odds are that 20% of your pages or products drive 80% of your visits and sales. If you try to focus on everything, you end up focusing on nothing," he adds.

Scoop #89: Content optimization – authority-ship

The best tip from Mat Siltala (alalaunchmedia.com) is on authority-ship, All content you publish – videos, slide decks, graphics, plain old "written content", etc. – needs to be associated with your Google Authorship and set-up correctly from a technical standpoint." The #1 mistake people make is to post images without text. Mat points out that the caption is needed to help the search engine know what the graphic is all about.

Scoop #90: Content optimization – design

The look of your content is a major factor when it comes to getting people to pay attention to your brand. The design and layout will either invite people to engage or make them run away. If the design is cluttered and unclear in terms of what you're talking about and what they can get out of it, people will be confused. If the type is hard to read or the links don't work, people won't bother with it. Great design looks really simple. You'd probably say, "I could have done that!" Chances are that a lot went into reducing it to its' basic essence.

One thing to keep in mind when you arrange the content of your post, blog, or website pages is to leave enough space around elements so the eye gets relief. Too much cramming is a negative because there are no breaks. Make contrast your friend because the eye can focus better on an element that is different. You can create contrast with space, images, typefaces, color, and layout. For example, a title that has one letter flipped in a word gets a

---

* Words & phrases underlined (links) are cross-referenced with URL addresses at the back

second look. You just have to check it. Patterns are a great way to lead the eye to the focal point.

Another thing to keep in mind is that "less is more". If you can say it with one word, don't use two. There's a lot of discussion about how long a blog should be or how long a title should be. Use as many words as you need and no more. There are top designers that make a headline three lines long and others that use one word – big and bold or miniscule.

One more thing, "show more and tell less". People engage more with visual content because it's brief and easy to absorb. A quote overlaid on a photo is a great example. Also, while we spend a lot of time in front of screens, research shows that it's harder to read long stories on them, except for e-readers.

There are basic elements of good design that you can learn in order to make your content look awesome and draw people to your brand. In general, aim for crispness and clarity in everything you do:

1. Branding elements – colors, fonts, and images have to be applied consistently across your content assets in order to create a unique style and a memorable brand
2. Images and filters – pick the ones that have an instant magnetic pull and tell a visual story that creates empathy, intrigue, or amazement
   - Crop an image tightly around the subject for interest and definition
   - Group smaller images together for impact – don't scatter them about on a page
   - Use monochromatic (any one color) tones for drama
   - Use images to break up text and give the eye focus

- Apply filters to your photos to create a consistent palette and tone
- Up the contrast level to bring out texture and separate blends
- Up the saturation level to add intensity and enhance colors
- Tweak highlights and shadows for contrast

3. Colors – pick 3 or 4 colors to depict your brand - at least one light and one dark tone for contrast. Visit colourlovers.com for inspiration. Colors are associated with certain feelings or moods and have traditional ties:

- Green stands for freshness and natural; it's used in the food industry (unprocessed, organic) and for green products (environment, recycle)
- Blue stands for security, loyalty, integrity and harmony; it's used to represent technology
- Yellow stands for happiness and joy; it's a warm color that gets the most attention
- Orange stands for friendship and adventure; it's used in sports a lot
- Red stands for passion, emergency, sexuality and lust; in eastern cultures it represents good luck
- Purple stands for independence, individuality, and inspiration; it's used to represent spirituality and magic
- Pink stands for romance and love; it's used to represent nurturing and compassion
- Gray stands for neutrality; it's an impartial color with no emotion

4. Fonts – pick 2 or 3 fonts for your brand with contrasting typefaces for impact, such as a sans serif and a serif. Learn to pair fonts to create harmony and not confusion. Don't

---

* Words & phrases underlined (links) are cross-referenced with URL addresses at the back

mix too many fonts and font sizes. Use type size to show hierarchy and organization.

5. Templates – make design easy. Every good designer uses templates to save time and stick to the same style and layout. There are apps and tools that make design easy:
   - canva.com has templates for Instagram, Twitter and Facebook posts; there's hundreds of designs for business cards, post cards, presentations, and free brand-kit templates
   - picmonkey.com allows you to design and create content
   - PowerPoint can be used to create infographics, charts, and posts
   - Slideshare can be used for presentations
   - Google+ has photo-enhancement and optimization tools
   - Google+ has popup cards you can use to send out invitations and manage events (registration, promotion via trailers, collect photos in albums, questions, etc.)
   - Google Docs can be used for surveys (design and data collection)

6. Google Photos is Google's brand new photo service for photo management. According to David Nield you can:
   - share an image or group of images through a link
   - use the intelligent search function to get suggestions on the web
   - send videos to YouTube
   - back up photos from other apps
   - make stories from your photos – a guided album with captions and locations
   - strip out geo-location data
   - import photos from computers and cameras
   - view photos and videos in Google Drive

- download photos to the desktop

7. To craft visual content, you'll have to get familiar with photo editing tools. This is a list of some popular tools. Use your own images or download from one of the many online sites:

- Photoshop – has lots of features and is used by most of the pros | www.photoshop.com
- HDR darkroom | www.everimaging.com/
- Fotor – powerful photo editing site | www.fotor.com/
- Sumopaint – online photo editing tool. Free for basic version; less than $5/month for pro version. Your browser has to support Flash | www.sumopaint.com
- GIMP – best free alternative to Photoshop. Runs on Windows, Mac OS X, Linux | www.gimp.org
- Paint – easier to use than Photoshop but only runs on Windows. Limited functions but useful for simple photo editing | Paint.net
- Pixlr – browser-based photo editing software, which uses Flash. Very easy to use, perfect for simple edits and no download required. Also available for smartphones | www.pixlr.com
- PixBuilder Studio – photo editor for professional use. Similar to GIMP but fewer features, so it's easier to use | www.wnsoft.com/pixbuilder/
- Image sharing and downloading sites – royalty-free images for non-commercial and commercial use (most free sites require that you add a credit link when you use the image)
  - www.shutterstock.com
  - www.gettyimages.ca
  - www.istockphoto.com

* Words & phrases underlined (links) are cross-referenced with URL addresses at the back

8. If you need the professional services of creative people, you can check out these sites:

- 99design.ca is an online marketplace where you fill out an online brief and choose a design package. After paying pay a contest is launched among graphics designers to create your design. A bigger prize attracts more designers. After 7 days, you pick the winning design.

- Fiverr.com is an online marketplace where designers, producers, web developers and other people advertise their services starting at $5.00 a gig. You often have to buy more gigs and pay much more depending on your project.

Scoop #91: Content optimization – need

The best tip from Monica Wright (marketingland.com) is to create content that meets the needs of the people you are trying to attract. Content is meant to be experienced. You can entertain, teach, or empathize. Start by answering five questions:

1. How do I…
2. What is…
3. Where can I find…
4. What's the best…
5. Who is…

Monica says the #1 mistake people make is to design a site and plug in content as an afterthought. She says that if you think of content as a benefit, you've got the backbone of a marketing plan. As a footnote, she adds, "People don't like to think. You need to show them."

Scoop #92: Content headlines

A clear and relevant headline or title is the most important thing you can do to ensure that your content gets read and shared. When it's good, it's click-worthy. David Ogilvy is quoted as saying that, "on the average, five times as many people read the headline as read the body copy. When you have written your headline, you have spent eighty cents out of your dollar."

Susanna Gebauer's blog on "How One Headline Can Make or Break Your Content Marketing Success" says that Upworthy, the website that is in the business of putting new headlines on old news, comes up with 25 different headlines for each piece of content. Why 25? Because that's what it takes for you to get really creative, and the last five will get you thinking differently. What tips does Upworthy offer?

- Don't say it all in the headline
- Don't be shrill
- Don't (over) sexualize
- Don't overthink

Pick five out of the 25 headlines, sleep on it, and then pick one. You may want to experiment with all five to see which one gets the most shares. Remember that posting at different times of the day affects the results.

To help you come up with ideas for 25 headlines, Susanna suggests relying on the experience of top bloggers "because there's a pattern for what works and what does not. Some types of headlines seem to resonate better with a social audience than others." Jeff Bullas analyzed which kinds of headlines work best for his blog and came up with a list:

* Words & phrases underlined (links) are cross-referenced with URL addresses at the back

1. Lists – "The 10 biggest things in the world"
2. How to's – "How to craft magnetic headlines"
3. Get-what-you-want headlines – "The secret to making money blogging"
4. Best or worst headlines – "The easiest way to get signups from Twitter" (Susanna says Jeff Bullas claims that negative headlines work best)
5. Statistics, facts and figures – sports scores, research data, etc.
6. Predictions – "Marketing trends you should not ignore"

Nick Churick reminds us of the simple fact that a headline will either motivate a person to click and read the post or ignore it. In a guest blog titled, "How to Leave your Readers no Other Choice but to Tweet your Content" he writes that a poor-headlined post will not even be opened; and on Twitter, it may be the only information a person ever sees.

*"If you have an awesome headline and it catches attention, some people will retweet it even without checking the article itself – just because they like your headline **that much**."*

— @Nick Churick

For advice on how to create a magnetic headline, Nick suggests reading the Headline Hacks Report, created by Jon Morrow. Another tip for Twitter headlines, is to keep it short (use about 100 of the 140 characters) in order to leave room for people to comment when retweeting your posts.

There are <u>handy formulas for writing headlines</u> but it's helpful to know what words and topics do well. Then you can optimize the headline and come up with content ideas that will attract and intrigue your target audience.

In the case of your blog and website pages, keep in mind that the headline/title also determines in part if your post is found in search results. If Google doesn't get it, you've wasted your time because the item won't show up in search results. Consider keywords, keyword phrases, and the order in which they appear.

You can decide on the headline after you craft the content but make sure it's a good one. Otherwise you'll be doing a postmortem ☺

Scoop #93: Marketing collateral

When you put a lot of effort into engaging your followers and leading them to your site, you don't want to lose them at that stage. Your site should present the information that a visitor needs to make a decision to purchase. If they are frustrated, they will leave.

Apparently some sites are missing content that visitors look for and that means they're not getting all their questions answered. There's an infographic at copyblogger.com that shows the "Marketing collateral most lacking on vendor websites". Customers need to be convinced that your claims are valid and the best way is with case studies, white papers, and articles. You want customers to make a purchase so they need pricing information. Product reviews, testimonials, and client lists impart confidence which you cannot convey. Shipping is a detail of concern to purchasers so it needs to be addressed. News releases, locations, and CAD drawings put the purchaser at ease.

---

* Words & phrases underlined (links) are cross-referenced with URL addresses at the back

Scoop #94: YouTube & Hangouts On Air – traffic & SEO

With over one billion active viewers per month, you don't want to ignore the YouTube platform for marketing and social networking. Google+ Hangouts On Air and YouTube can help you produce your videos. But with over 100 hours of video uploaded per minute, you have to be smart about producing content which grabs viewers and keeps them coming back to your channel. First, they have to find your video, which means you have to get on top of the Google Search page. Scott Buehler has produced a detailed guide which covers all the bases, "YouTube Guide to Traffic and SEO" at scottbuehler.com. The basic guidelines are as follows:

1. Keep the video short – 3 to 5 minutes retains viewers and gives you added benefits for Google Search
2. Optimize your file for upload – name your file with keywords in mind
3. Optimize your video title – put primary keywords in the title starting with the most important
4. Write a video description – at least two paragraphs and include secondary keywords. Google Search uses this for relevancy. Assume the viewer will read this before deciding to watch the video. Also list other videos you may have on your channel. You can also create a playlist and link that in your description. That's another search plus.
5. Use the best keyword tags – keywords that the viewer would use to search for your video content. Add as many tags as you can. Your primary and secondary keywords should go into your tags. Put the primary at the beginning of the list. Put the video ID among the tags and if you have room find popular and relevant videos in your niche and add their ID's too.

6. Add close captions – not only is it vital for the hearing impaired but if the speaker is hard to understand, closed captions help. Also, Google's advanced filtering options help people search for videos with closed captions. This may help improve your relevancy score, which means your video might rank for obscure but related content and get on the search page.

7. Share your video immediately – promote it to as many people as you can; on on as many sites as you can; and in as many ways as you can (email links, blogs, Google+ posts, Twitter, Facebook, Pinterest, etc.)

8. Create a playlist – the more playlists, the better. Base them on your niches or interests. Google indexes each playlist giving your videos more chances to be found.

9. Ask and you shall receive – At the end of your video tell viewers what you want them to do exactly: subscribe, leave a comment, and thumbs up. Asks questions and ask for shares on social media.

10. Build your subscribers – Be consistent. Provide epic value. Use video annotations to create a call to action and ask for subscribers.

11. Engage people on YouTube – when you take the time to comment on other people's videos, you are advertising your name and spreading awareness about your YouTube channel and Profile. Each time you comment, your name is linked and it points to your Google+ Profile, giving people a chance to find you. Also, other people might stumble on your channel because of your comments.

Scoop #95: How to write great blog posts

Debbie Hemley is an expert when it comes to content marketing. Her blog, "26 Tips for Writing Great Blog Posts" is an excellent resource of curated content and useful tips which are not widely written about:

1. Make it anatomically correct – that's how you optimizes it for conversion – Pamela Seiple outlines six points to focus on
2. Blogging platform – master and keep on top of updates
3. Categories – choose categories and stick to them for clarity
4. Description – create a meta-description less than 160 characters for Search
5. Editorial calendar – schedule and organize topics for blogs but use a spreadsheet with tags, per Michele Linn
6. Fine tune and revise – revise and edit as much as needed before publishing
7. Guidelines for writing for search engines – increase the chance of being found by Search engines, especially Google. The State University of New York at Plattsburgh suggests sticking to what Google likes: text, formatting, freshness, accessibility, outbound hyperlinks, link your pages, tell it where you are, and experts.
8. Headings – define which parts of your content are most important and how they're inter-connected, and structure is very important for on-page SEO. Joost de Valk offers five basic principles for heading structure. Use H1 for the most important heading and H2s and H3s for subheadings and sub-subheadings. Each heading should contain valuable keywords. For longer blogs, headings help readers skip to what they find interesting.

9. Images – increase readership and blog views. Judy Dunn offers 5 ways that photos do this: convey feeling, illustrates an idea with a metaphor or analogy, evokes surprise or curiosity, complements headline, makes readers smile.

10. Journalistic Approach – is the way that journalists approach news stories. Mickie Kennedy offers five things bloggers can learn from journalists:

    a. get your facts straight
    b. trust is earned
    c. credit sources
    d. use the inverted pyramid to write
    e. edit and proofread

    The inverted pyramid starts with most newsworthy info in the first paragraph, then gives important details, and ends with general info and background.

11. Killer SEO and blog design – elements which add to a blog's success are found in infographic by Cyrus Shepard:

    - Search box
    - RSS feed
    - Breadcrumbs (helping users navigate)
    - Flat site architecture by minimizing the number of clicks it takes to reach your content
    - Images
    - Keep your best content above the fold
    - Link to your best content
    - Don't overdo links
    - Watch ad space
    - Encourage comments
    - Add sharing buttons
    - Test the blog for speed
    - Check your blog in different browsers

* Words & phrases underlined (links) are cross-referenced with URL addresses at the back

- Pick a powerhouse blogging platform (e.g., WordPress, Posterous, Tumblr)

12. Lists – popular style of blog posts. Nate Riggs offers three types for bloggers to consider: brief, detailed and hybrid lists. Every bullet of a detailed list is a complete thought. Nate suggests focusing on quality rather than quantity.

13. Metrics for blogging – measure performance to determine what is working and what interests your readers most. Magdalena Georgieva identifies five metrics: visitors, leads, subscribers, inbound links and social media shares.

14. Name, title, and bio – background info which can add clout and put readers at ease.

15. Original vs. curated content – while original is presumed to be better, Pamela Seiple "it takes time and careful evaluation to create quality curated content". The result can save readers time.

16. Publish and Promote – be sure to have a clear call to action. What do you want people to do after they read your post? Kristi Hines has a different plan for average-awesome posts, awesome posts, and killer-awesome posts. The plan differs in terms of promotion: how many social networks she shares the posts with, whether she includes the post in her writing portfolio, and whether it's included in her custom RSS feed or utilizes blog commenting promotion and direct messaging partners in social media to see if they'll help spread the word.

17. Questions – use them to come up with topics for your blogs. Lee Odden suggests reviewing web analytics for the kinds of questions people type into search engines like Google or Bing.

18. Research – become the go-to resource in your industry. Well-researched topics make your blogs stand out. Oli

Gardner suggests using social media for your research, involving these 10 strategies:

a. StumbleUpon
b. Infographics
c. Twitter real-time searches
d. Facebook events
e. Experts who are using LinkedIn
f. Uncovering quotes with Delicious
g. Letting users tell you within the comments section of your blog and others
h. Creating roundup mega-lists with Delicious and StumbleUpon
i. Apps on Facebook
j. Delicious and Google Marketplace
k. YouTube and the UrbanDictionary

19. Stand out – use others' blogs to differentiate your own. Just because someone has already written about your topic, doesn't mean you have to abandon it. Use the other posts that are similar to yours to learn what to imitate and what to improve on. The questions and thoughts in the comments can help you take a slightly different approach to your blog.

20. Title – very important to grab attention, send a full message to the intended audience, and lure them into the body text. Brian Clark writes that the title is the first, and perhaps only, impression you make on a prospective reader.

21. User-centered content – write for your readers, their needs, and their interests. Georgy Cohen says the content can serve as customer service and to be helpful, content should be user-focused (asking what our users' problems

---

* Words & phrases underlined (links) are cross-referenced with URL addresses at the back

and priorities are), communicated clearly and presented in succinct language.

22. Valuable content – step-by-step checklist created by Ahava Leibtag that reminds us to ask five questions:

    a. Can the user find the content
    b. Can the user read the content
    c. Can the user understand the content
    d. Will the user want to take action
    e. Will the user share the content

What makes content valuable?

- It's findable – includes an H1 tag; at least two H2 tags; metadata including title, descriptors and keywords; links to other related content; ALT tags for images
- It's readable – has an inverted-pyramid writing style, chunking, bullets, numbered lists, following the style guide
- It's understandable – an appropriate content type (text, video), indication that you considered the users' persona, context, respect for the users' reading level, articulating an old idea in a new way
- It's actionable – has a call to action, a place to comment, an invitation to share, links to related content, a direct summary of what to do
- It's shareable – provokes an emotional response, a reason to share, a request to share, an easy way to share, personalization

23. Word count – how long should it be? Some blogs want an optimal length and track it as either short or long. Corey Eridon suggests that we may be overly pre-occupied, "Some topics take 100 words to explain, some take 1,000, and that's okay." Writers should focus instead on whether posts are optimized for mobile, use effective formatting,

and communicate in a clear manner. Outlining the points you want to make is ultimately better use of your time and energy. For shorter posts, you may want to link to longer-form content developed arount the topic. The point is don't let the quantity of posts compromise quality.

24. (E)xcerpt – A shorter post can be an excerpt or summary of longer-form content, used strategically for click-through. You could post an excerpt of an e-book or white paper. But an excerpt doesn't have to be restricted to words. An excerpt of a transcript or a brief description to demonstrate what users can learn by watching your video or listening to your podcast.

25. Your Story – It's been mentioned before that readers are curious and interested in personal details. Business blogs are not supposed to be a personal diary but the reader wants details and insights about the topic from the person "who has taken them on a journey through a post". You can tell your readers about how you operate and how your post fits into your repertoire. If you can mix a bit of the personal with the business angle, you "humanize" the story. After all we're human – not robots.

26. Zone for writing –While ideas flow all the time – day and night – it helps if you follow a routine that keeps interruptions to a minimum. Create a time and place where you can get into the zone and just write. Try not to edit as you go. Finish your first draft and then edit and re-edit.

---

* Words & phrases underlined (links) are cross-referenced with URL addresses at the back

Extra Scoops

Scoop #96: Top G+ tipsters

There is a team of "top G+ tipsters" that you need to follow in order to stay on top of Google+ and social media. The content they post is fantastic and will inform and keep you up-to-date. This is the short list of who they are – you'll find them all on Google+:

+martin shervington   +Christine DeGraff

+Brian Jensen   +Ryan Hanley

+Denis Labelle   +Rick Eliason

+Guy Kawasaki   +Stephan Hovnanian

+Jaana Nyström   +Ben Fisher

+Mark Traphagen   +Ronnie Bincer

Scoop #97: Where to go to learn more

There are many fabulous resources online and I've reviewed lots of them in this book. You'll also find a long list in my book "Cut to the Chase: The Best Sites to Learn How to Build & Sell Online". There are some fantastic sites that offer a buffet of content. This is a very short list chosen randomly:

- Social Media Examiner
- Hubspot Blog
- buffersocial
- Krishna inforgraphics
- Business2Community
- Entrepreneur

For example, the Social Media Examiner is "Your Guide to the Social Media Jungle". You'll find marketing tips and tricks related to social media networks – Facebook, LinkedIn, Instagram, etc. Their lineup of articles published from June 24 – 30, 2015 included:

1. How to Use LinkedIn Publisher Statistics to Refine Your Marketing
2. How to Craft Instagram Posts That Drive Sales
3. Ways to Track Your Social Media Marketing Activities
4. Facebook Advertising Tools That Save Time and Improve Your ROI
5. How to Craft Instagram Posts That Drive Sales
6. Snapchat Native Video Ads: This Week in Social Media
7. Facebook Groups: How to Nurture a Community on Facebook
8. How to Use Facebook Custom Audiences for Increased Reach
9. Win Free Membership in Social Media Marketing Society

Scoop #98: Boost your content marketing with Facebook's MPAs – for free

Alan Coleman's blog, 8 Ways Content Marketers Can Hack Facebook Multi-Product Ads can boost engagement for your content while saving you money. Facebook's Multi-Product Ads (MPAs) are designed to promote products on the platform similarly to Google Shopping. But Alan says this is the wrong way

* Words & phrases underlined (links) are cross-referenced with URL addresses at the back

for Facebook to monetize the site because users are not there to buy but to share. Because users are hungry for content, you can format MPAs to promote content rather than products and all the shares, likes, and comments are free.

Alan shares eight ways that MPA Hacks have worked well for his business, Wolfgang Digital, an award winning marketer in Europe. Switching the case use of Multi-Product Ads to Multi-Content Ads is indeed an inventive hack. MPA's allow retailers to split the frame and show multiple products.

It's a terrific format that you can leverage to guide users to relevant content and boost engagement, and it's simple to do:

"We attempted to see if Facebook Ads Manager would accept MPAs promoting content rather than products. We plugged in the images, copy and landing pages, hit "place order", and lo and behold the ads became active. We're happy to say that the engagement rates, and more importantly the amplification rates, are fantastic!" – **Alan Coleman**

This technique allows you to promote multiple pieces of content simultaneously. Bundling content and delivering it in this smart format, is a clever way to target Facebook's massive audience:

"...it's no secret that Facebook's organic reach continues to dwindle. The cold commercial reality is you need to pay to play on FB. The good news is that if you select 'website clicks' as your objective you only pay for website traffic and engagement while amplification by likes, comments, and shares are free! Those website clicks you pay for are typically substantially cheaper than Adwords, Taboola, Outbrain, Twitter or LinkedIn. How does it compare to display? It doesn't. Paying for clicks is always preferable to paying for impressions. If you are spending money on display advertising I'd urge you to fling a few spondoolas towards Facebook ads and compare results. You will be pleasantly surprised."

– Alan Coleman

You could use MPA Hacks to promote multiple packages, locations, people, events, UGCs, programs, training, tours, etc. As an example, the first MPA Hack case use shared by Alan promotes various travel packages.

Consider MPA Hacks as a valuable tool for promoting your content on Facebook. Allan comments that, "AdWords is still the best ad platform in the world for conversion. While Facebook can rival it for reach, relevance and CPCs it can't come close on conversion (in most cases)." So use it for reach, relevance and CPCs. If you're already paying for advertising, this is an extra boost to engagement that you get for free.

Index of Top Social Media Networks

So-o-Good: Endnotes

Thank you for purchasing a copy of this book!

1. **Help me out:** I sincerely hope that my I-SPY Insider's Edition of "Social Media Marketing Strategy" was a rewarding read. I would greatly appreciate your feedback with an honest review on Amazon.com. It can be as brief as one word or a paragraph or two. First and foremost, I'm always looking to grow and improve as a writer. It is reassuring to hear what works, as well as receive constructive feedback on what should improve. Second, starting out as an unknown author is exceedingly difficult, and Amazon reviews go a long way toward making the journey out of anonymity possible. Please take a few minutes to write an honest review. Best regards, Alex Abaz

2. **Bonus offers:**
   As a verified purchaser, I would be most pleased to email you an enhanced version of this book in pdf format. It includes numerous graphics and that's another layer of information that will improve learning. Also, for those of you who bought the paperback version, the pdf file has the advantage of navigation links. To receive the file, please email me at so.o.good.productions@gmail.com using the subject line: *I-SPY Insider's Edition – Enhanced bonus offer*
   Upon receiving your email I will add you to my Readers' List so you receive updates and advance review copies for free.

3. Some of my books are available exclusively at:
   http://sites.google.com/site/publishdigitally/

4. Join me on social media:
   a. twitter.com/Alex_Abaz [@Alex_Abaz]
   b. google.com/+SooGoodAlex [+So-o-Good]
   c. facebook.com/Alex.Abaz.Author

* Words & phrases underlined (links) are cross-referenced with URL addresses at the back

Cross-Reference of Hidden Links (URL Addresses)

Brian Clark: http://www.copyblogger.com/how-to-write-headlines-that-work/

brief description to demonstrate: http://www.socialmediaexaminer.com/how-small-businesses-should-adapt-to-social-media/
BufferSocial: http://blog.bufferapp.com/best-time-to-tweet-research

Business2Community: http://www.business2community.com/

BuzzFeed's: http://www.adweek.com/socialtimes/cute-or-not-buzzfeed-launches-animal-photo-sharing-app-on-ios/616075
BuzzSumo: http://buzzsumo.com/

Chloe's blog: http://blog.kissmetrics.com/create-winning-marketing-surveys/

content analysis: http://www.quora.com/Wayne-Liew

Content Explorer: http://ahrefs.com/content-explorer

ConversionXL: http://conversionxl.com/

Corey Eridon:
http://blog.hubspot.com/http:/blog.hubspot.com/blog/tabid/6307/bid/28730/Why-Focusing-on-Blog-Word-Count-Is-Stupid.aspxblog/tabid/6307/bid/28730/Why-Focusing-on-Blog-Word-Count-Is-Stupid.aspx
Create a Great Site & Have it Found in Google:
http://plus.google.com/b/112167523804907029932/+DenisLabelle/posts/cY692heKNb1
"Cut to the Chase: The Best Sites to Learn How to Build & Sell Online":
http://www.amazon.com/Chase-sites-online-digital-videos-ebook/dp/B00QG5Y8SS
Danny Wong: http://disqus.com/by/disqus_GPAIJhSsbD/

David Ogilvy: http://blog.hubspot.com/marketing/common-keyword-data

David Nield: http://fieldguide.gizmodo.com/tag/google-photos

demographic data: http://www.facebook.com/help/118314051609562

Douglas Mason: http://twitter.com/CaliCoyote

eBiz MBA: http://www.ebizmba.com/articles/social-networking-websites

eight times:
http://cdn2.hubspot.net/hub/53/blog/docs/ebooks/the_2012_state_of_inbound_marketing.pdf
Entrepreneur: http://www.entrepreneur.com/

Facebook events: http://www.facebook.com/help/events

Facebooks's competitive report:
http://freereports.simplymeasured.com/viewer/3lp68gm7bmpy4idbqm7vn5m5racwfm/1047020
Forrester: http://www.forrester.com/The+Case+For+Google+Plus/fulltext/-/-E-RES113003?aid=AST967719#AST967719
Freelance Writer: http://kristihines.com/

Georgy Cohen: http://meetcontent.com/blog/2011/09/content-as-customer-service/

Google Analytics: http://www.socialmediaexaminer.com/new-google-analytics-features/

Google authorship: http://www.socialmediaexaminer.com/google-author-tags/

Google's brand new photo service: http://gizmodo.com/google-photos-hands-on-so-good-im-creeped-out-1707566376
Google Marketplace: http://www.google.com/enterprise/marketplace/?pli=1

Google Publisher: http://wordpress.org/plugins/google-publisher/

Government & Politics: http://media.twitter.com/best-practice/government-politics-what-works-best/

Headline Hacks Report : http://boostblogtraffic.com/headline-hacks/

headlines work best for his blog : http://www.jeffbullas.com/2013/08/21/10-awesome-headlines-that-drive-traffic-and-attracts-readers

holistic approach: http://www.quora.com/What-is-the-best-way-to-promote-content-on-the-web: http://www.quora.com/What-is-the-best-way-to-promote-content-on-the-web

Hubspot Blog: http://blog.hubspot.com/blog/tabid/6307/bid/18340/The-Simple-Anatomy-of-a-Conversion-Optimized-Blog.aspx

HubSpot: http://www.hubspot.com/

iElectirfy: http://ielectrify.com/about-me

Images and photos: http://b2b-marketing-mentor.softwareadvice.com/study-how-marketers-optimize-social-content-0614/

infographic: http://www.seomoz.org/img/upload/killer-blog-design.jpg

Innovation Report: http://www.adweek.com/fishbowlny/editorial-analytics-the-missing-link-in-monetization/269182

Instagram, Twitter and Facebook :
http://www.canva.com/design/DABWckO6bcw/vZB2JoYzXEHPOyVQS
http://www.canva.com/design/DABWchAfdrI/r_We-QptpPHc3oWULi3Ziw/edit

http://www.canva.com/design/DABWclWkygk/jRG3vijhuLolyOcInE

Instantly Irresistible: http://howtobeinstantlyirresistible.com/

Interactive content: http://www.demandgenreport.com/industry-topics/content-strategies/2746-b2b-content-preferences-survey-buyers-want-short-visual-mobile-optimized-content.html

Jesse Mawhinney: http://blog.hubspot.com/marketing/author/jesse-mawhinney

Joost de Valk: http://yoast.com/blog-headings-structure/

KISSmetrics: http://www.kissmetrics.com/

Krishna inforgraphics: http://krishnainfographics.com/

Kristi Hines: http://www.incomediary.com/creating-a-successful-blog-post-from-idea-to-promotion

Learn more: http://support.google.com/adwords/answer/3236114

Lee Odden: http://www.toprankblog.com/2011/10/blog-content-questions/

links: http://www.adweek.com/socialtimes/news-feed-click-baiting-link-format/437351

Locowise: http://locowise.com/

Louis Vuitton: http://www.internetretailer.com/2014/03/03/pre-owned-sales-soar-online

Lynnette Young: http://lynetteyoung.com/

Magdalena Georgieva: http://blog.hubspot.com/blog/tabid/6307/bid/29315/5-Critical-Metrics-to-Measure-Business-Blog-Performance.aspx

many marketers : [many] http://comprendia.com/2012/08/01/are-40-of-life-science-company-facebook-page-likes-from-fake-users/ and [marketers] http://blog.pubchase.com/what-do-facebook-likes-of-companies-mean/

many publishers : [many] http://www.businessinsider.in/This-Mans-600000-Ad-Disaster-On-Facebook-Is-A-Warning-For-All-Small-Business-Owners/articleshow/30867015.cms / [and [publishers] http://www.youtube.com/watch?v=oVfHeWTKjag

Markitekt: http://www.markitekt.com/

Michael Steizner: http://www.socialmediaexaminer.com/google-marketing-tactics-promote-

---

* Words & phrases underlined (links) are cross-referenced with URL addresses at the back

content-google/

Michele Linn : http://www.contentmarketinginstitute.com/2010/08/content-marketing-editorial-calendar/
Mickie Kennedy: http://www.ereleases.com/prfuel/5-things-bloggers-can-learn-from-journalists/

Music: http://media.twitter.com/best-practice/music-the-impact-of-tweeting-with-photos-videos-hashtags-and-links/
Nate Elliott's blog: http://blogs.forrester.com/nate_elliott/14-03-17-facebook_is_still_failing_marketers
Nate Riggs: http://www.contentmarketinginstitute.com/2011/06/blog-post-lists-for-content-marketing/
National Geographic: http://www.adweek.com/socialtimes/national-geographic-dominates-publishers-october-facebook-twitter-instagram-actions/439180
News: http://media.twitter.com/best-practice/news-the-impact-of-tweeting-with-photos-videos-hashtags-and-links/
NewsWhip: http://blog.newswhip.com/index.php/2015/03/different-content-different-facebook-interactions
niche: http://siteber.com/top-10-effective-ways-to-promote-your-content/

Nick Churig: http://blog.thesocialms.com/how-to-leave-your-readers-no-other-choice-but-to-tweet-your-content/
number one driver of referral traffic:
http://www.forbes.com/sites/jaysondemers/2015/02/03/social-media-now-drives-31-of-all-referral-traffic/
Ogilvy released data: http://adage.com/article/digital/brands-organic-facebook-reach-crashed-october/292004/
Oli Gardner: http://unbounce.com/social-media/10-social-media-research-strategies-to-enhance-your-next-blog-post/
one of the most lucrative grifts of all time: http://digiday.com/platforms/facebook-agencies/

ongoing effort: http://newsroom.fb.com/news/category/news-feed-fyi/

original visual content:
http://www.socialmediaexaminer.com/SocialMediaMarketingIndustryReport2014.pdf
Page publishing tips and best practices: http://www.facebook.com/business/a/page-posting-tips

Pamela Seiple: http://blog.hubspot.com/blog/tabid/6307/bid/18340/The-Simple-Anatomy-of-a-Conversion-Optimized-Blog.aspx
Politico: http://www.adweek.com/socialtimes/mashable-jim-roberts-outraged-politico-apocalypsticles/144524
Posts with photos: http://www.emarketer.com/Article/Photos-Cluttering-Your-Facebook-Feed-Herersquos-Why/1010777/1#sthash.nJwqhFkr.dpuf
RedEnvelope: http://plus.google.com/+redenvelope/posts

released a new Creator playbook for brands: http://www.webpronews.com/youtube-gives-brands-their-own-creator-playbook-2014-03
research shows: http://searchengineland.com/eye-tracking-study-everybody-looks-at-organic-listings-but-most-ignore-paid-ads-on-right-67698
Review extensions: http://support.google.com/trustedstoresmerchant/answer/6081510?hl=en

reviews: http://searchengineland.com/adwords-new-review-extensions-beta-tests-third-party-blurbs-in-ads-165130
shares: http://www.adweek.com/socialtimes/newswhip-november-2014/439979

Social Media Examiner: http://www.socialmediaexaminer.com/

Social signals: http://kaiserthesage.com/social-signals

Source: http://www.quora.com/Whats-the-difference-between-marketing-automation-and-inbound-marketing

Spike: http://spike.newswhip.com/welcome

Sports: http://media.twitter.com/best-practice/sports-the-impact-of-tweeting-with-photos-videos-hashtags-and-links
status updates: http://www.adweek.com/socialtimes/feeling-fat/616606

StumbleUpon: http://www.stumbleupon.com/?

Susanna Gebauer: http://blog.thesocialms.com/author/susanna-gebauergooglemail-com/

syndication: http://goo.gl/EVOsmR

The Atlantic: http://www.adweek.com/socialtimes/zuckerberg-atlantic/428547

the Author Tag: http://media.fb.com/2015/06/18/using-author-tags-to-grow-your-audience/

the fourth top Internet activity: http://mashable.com/2013/08/15/popular-online-activities/

The State University of New York at Plattsburgh:
http://www.plattsburgh.edu/intranet/webresources/seo.php
Thomasnet: http://www.thomasnet.com/

Tim Ash: http://marketingland.com/author/tim-ash

time spent reading: http://www.socialmediatoday.com/social-business/adhutchinson/2015-06-14/facebook-updates-news-feed-instant-articles-gain-more-reach
TMZ: http://www.adweek.com/socialtimes/joan-rivers-iphone-6-scheduled-post/437917

Tweets with images: http://blog.bufferapp.com/the-power-of-twitters-new-expanded-images-and-how-to-make-the-most-of-it
Twitter Blog: http://blog.twitter.com/2014/what-fuels-a-tweets-engagement

Twitter real-time searches: http://tweettabs.com/

Upworthy : http://www.upworthy.com/

UrbanDictionary: http://www.urbandictionary.com/

use your Audience to create an ad: http://www.facebook.com/help/800555799956232

Venchito Tampon: http://digitalphilippines.net/11-off-page-seo-strategies-to-get-more-website-traffic/
video posts: http://blog.bufferapp.com/the-power-of-twitters-new-expanded-images-and-how-to-make-the-most-of-it
videos: http://www.adweek.com/socialtimes/buzzfeed-ze-frank-facebook-auto-play-videos/615451
Visual content: http://blog.hubspot.com/marketing/visual-content-marketing-strategy

Why we like, share, comment on Facebook: http://cdn2.hubspot.net/hub/53/hubfs/Why-We-Like-Share-Comment-on-Facebook-infographic.jpg?t=1435668631938&width=669
your posts: http://www.facebook.com/help/336143376466063

---

* Words & phrases underlined (links) are cross-referenced with URL addresses at the back